How to Profit
in Precious
Metals

How to Profit in Precious Metals

JACOB BERNSTEIN

A Wiley-Interscience Publication

JOHN WILEY & SONS

New York • Chichester • Brisbane • Toronto • Singapore

Library of Congress Cataloging in Publication Data:

Bernstein, Jacob, 1946–
    How to profit in precious metals.

    "A Wiley Interscience publication."
    Bibliography: p.
    Includes index.
    1. Commodity exchanges—Handbooks, manual, etc.
2. Precious metals—Handbooks, manuals, etc.   3. Copper
industry and trade—Finance—Handbooks, manuals, etc.
I. Title.
HG6046.B393   1985   332.64′5   84-19561
ISBN 0-471-88746-3

Printed in the United States of America

10 9 8 7 6 5 4 3 2 1

In memory of my dear departed mother, Sara,
who taught me that persistence, patience,
and a positive attitude are more precious
than silver or gold . . .

Preface

For many years I have been a student of price cycles. I have watched many futures traders frustrate themselves, while they attempted to trade short-term cyclic patterns in the futures markets. I have also watched professional traders (investors and commercial interests) make large profits by taking long-term positions consistent with secular trends of given markets. It occurred to me that someone should propose a system based on cyclic and historic precedent that would combine all the logical elements that must necessarily be part of a long-term investment approach. Consequently, I carefully studied historical patterns, cycles, trend characteristics, top and bottom formations, investor behavior, money management, and portfolio diversification to arrive at a logical technique by which the long-term trader can either accumulate positions, at or close to the bottom of major moves, or liquidate positions, at or close to the top of major moves. After acquiring the basics of this technique and after counseling my clients through numerous moves in the futures markets including, but not necessarily limited to, metals, I developed the technique into a logical methodology. My theoretical work has been subjected to sufficient public testing to warrant its advancement to the investment community.

In today's investment world minimal information is available to the long-term trader, because long-term trading is either discouraged or psychologically difficult to accomplish. Whereas the public believes that professionals favor such "investment objectives," the emotions of market behavior, and the violent price fluctuations, as well as the attitude of many brokers, often conflict with this goal. Only through the application of a disciplined approach that is well-planned, well-conceived, and well-organized will the chances for success increase. But success derives from total implementation of specific programs, not from partial implementation of various techniques—whether one is by nature a "technician" or a "fundamentalist." By proposing the program described in this text, I am offering you, in effect, a method that is the by-product of many years' experience in market analysis, trading, and investor counseling on an intensive, ongoing basis.

I cannot guarantee, of course, that this or any other approach to long-range investing will always be effective. Nevertheless, the concept of long-term investing will benefit if this work stimulates additional research and writing in this area. Perhaps, an additional by-product of this book will be more profitable long-term investment. As a market professional, I know that each approach to investment must be adapted to suit individual needs. In implementing the various aspects of the long-term investment program described in this text, you must always consider your particular financial situation. These needs are known only to you (and to your investment counselor), and general statements will not suffice in every situation. I, therefore, recommend that before implementing any information derived from your reading of this text, you examine it logically through studying historical market facts (i.e., price behavior or price history), and then decide for yourself whether the technique is potentially useful for your investment program. Although I have complete confidence in the techniques described, *you* are the one who must feel comfortable implementing the procedures.

Furthermore, long-term investment decisions are usually more suited to the time schedule of most individual investors. Moreover, long-term investing also tends to limit many negative emotions, such as fear, hope, greed, and frustration. Many successful investors and speculators through the years have reached the same conclusions based on their experiences with the market. Additional reasons for using a long-term approach are cited in the text that follows. Suffice it to say, therefore, that this book presupposes your interest in long-term trading. The principles outlined cannot necessarily be adapted to short-term trading, although they may have some merit in implementing intermediate-term trading programs. The tools offered in this text should be used strictly for the purposes stated and intended. To abuse or to subvert their intended function could cause you difficulty. Since I do not wish to be responsible for any problems such misuse may cause, I forewarn you that I do not recommend more than minor adaptations in or adjustments to the proposed techniques.

WHAT NOT TO EXPECT

It has often been said that expectation leads to disappointment. Perhaps this should be modified to read that *unrealistic* expectation leads to disappointment. I urge you, therefore, to have only modest expectations; not to expect instantaneous miracles; not to expect that every market and every move will conform to the rules; and not to expect complete understanding of the concepts without practice and rereading. To achieve success in this or in any other area requires effort, consistency, and *time*. If you know ahead of time that the achievement of investment success in the metals market requires the cultivation of certain qualities and habits, but the suppression of others, you will be more inclined to stay with the work. I caution you, therefore, to avoid any expectation that is either premature or inconsistent with the goals we have established. Follow the rules, and you will be pleased; violate the rules, and you *may* fail.

JACOB BERNSTEIN

Winnetka, Illinois
January 1985

Acknowledgments

I wish to thank personally the many people who helped make this book a reality. At my office, where things tend to get hectic every day, I appreciate the valuable managerial help of Marilyn Kinney. Thanks to Dolores Johnson who kept my subscriber list in order, James Pursley who entered the data and ran my fancy and not so fancy charts, and Ruth McConnell who organized and typed my manuscript. Those who granted permission to have their charts reproduced deserve a special note of thanks, in particular the Commodity Research Bureau and Mr. William Jiler whose years in the futures information area make him a true survivor. My two children receive special consideration for their always welcome assistance in using my original charts as scratch pads for their "scribble-scrabble" (suitable for framing). Jan Greene, my typist, has now successfully waded through my fourth manuscript (truly an achievement). Finally, my wife, Linda, who dislikes my writing books almost as much as I dislike writing them, deserves thanks for extra hours of baby-sitting while I baby-sat my typewriter.

J. B.

Contents

How to Profit
in Precious
Metals

Introduction

Gold and silver have played a significant role in the history of humanity. As a source of power and as a storehouse of wealth, precious metals have captured both the interest and the daydreams of investors for hundreds of years. If one were to take a deterministic view, it would be possible to rewrite world history as a cause and effect drama with humans' need to acquire silver and gold as the motivating force. Fortunately, however, the study of history has progressed to a level that no longer views human behavior from a deterministic focus. Yet the lure of metals, particularly the precious and rare variety, has been and still remains extremely intense; thus, to ignore the historical effects of the human quest for their possession would be to ignore a major historical force.

In addition, many other avenues of historical perspective also exist. One methodology, for example is cyclic price analysis. Thanks to the work of such pioneers as Edward R. Dewey and the Foundation for the Study of Cycles, our efforts to understand price cycles and their behavior have been made less difficult.* In this area, the metals have also attracted a considerable interest. The availability of lengthy historical data, particularly on copper, has made this market a prime target for cyclic studies. Lieutenant Commander David Williams has published a number of thorough cyclic studies on silver and gold prices,† and efforts to isolate key cyclic forces in precious metals continue in full force.

During the recent periods of severe inflation throughout the free world, precious metals have received even greater attention as vehicles for the preservation of capital. Notwithstanding the additional interest in metals during such crises as the OPEC oil embargo and the military intensification in the Middle East, few market analysts, economists, or investors have avoided analyzing

---

* Edward R. Dewey, *Cycles* (Pittsburgh: Foundation for the Study of Cycles, 1970).

† David Williams, "Cycles in Silver, Gold, and Economics," *Cycles,* May/June 1982.

and/or commenting on the precious metals. Despite the considerable interest in metals, however, few individuals, either professional or public have taken the time to study cyclic behavior in these markets.

For too long it has been taken for granted that precious metals will rise during periods of uncertainty and turmoil. It is, perhaps for this reason that investors and market professionals have paid minimal attention to the seasonality and cyclicality of metals. Consequently, they have ignored a powerful source of information—not to mention an equally significant source of profits. Of course many other avenues of analysis have been neither ineffective nor worthless. I believe, however, that their efforts have been less effective due to lack of attention to the important repetitive forces that have affected metals for hundreds of years.

Since my area of expertise in the markets has been primarily cyclic and seasonal analyses, I felt that it was important to apply my skills to the study of metals. My primary intentions, therefore, are to awaken public interest in metal cycles and to propose a theory that has pragmatic implications for the investor who might potentially profit from price fluctuations in the metals. I believe that the cyclic forces in metals prices can be delineated and visualized graphically and that the cycles, once known, can be used in the formulation of an investment program. I do not intend to prove the existence of cycles in metals, since this has already been done. Rather, my purpose is to explain in considerable detail my theoretical suggestions concerning how the cycles might be implemented, with profit as the ultimate goal.

To accomplish my goals, it was first necessary to formulate a few working definitions and then, with these definitions clearly in mind, to apply them functionally. Hence, it was necessary to structure this book similar to the way one would organize a textbook thereby optimizing the learning process. To many of you the concepts presented will be new, and several readings of certain sections and passages may be required. To those who were previously exposed to my ideas presented in *The Handbook of Commodity Cycles—A Window on Time,** what I say here will be familiar, though approached from a different perspective. To those who are familiar with my concepts of seasonality, what I have to say about this area relative to the metals will also be familiar, yet you will see that it is also approached from a different perspective. For those who have a limited understanding of repetitive price patterns, I will provide suggestions for further readings. This book, however, should serve as sufficient education, even for the novice, since I define and explain concepts when they are introduced.

My previous books and research studies were directed primarily at the futures market from an intermediate to a short-term perspective. Though I have made considerable mention of long-term trends and their immense value to the investor, I have not delineated a methodology that could translate study and theory into practice. What follows this book, however, should fill the void. I believe that the methods, suggestions, analyses, and guidelines presented in this book can stand alone and require no in-depth understanding of the inter-

---

* Jacob Bernstein, *The Handbook of Commodity Cycles—A Window on Time* (New York: John Wiley, 1981).

national political situation. Nor do they require a knowledge of fundamental analysis, the intricacies of metal refining, mining, monetary policy, or advanced economic theory. Because the student of cycles examines primarily price patterns in relation to time, little else does or should matter. In the final analysis whoever can determine when to buy and when to sell emerges as the victorious investor.

Some theorists create more heat than light, others create more fantasy than fact, and still others strive to be parsimonious in both their formulation and their application. It is with the last group that I belong. Consequently, you may find my explanations and conceptualizations simple. At times you may find them so simple that they become complex in their simplicity. Above all, remember that I have broken with tradition in presenting precious metals investing from a cyclic standpoint. Specifically, I have avoided the usual rhetoric about banking crises, world debt, hyperinflation, and so on. I see all of these factors as explanations for the movement of metals prices, but explanations develop after the fact. I maintain that the most fruitful avenue an investor can take is to *anticipate* periods of time during which prices should change direction. After the anticipated time frame has been entered, one can apply various technical tools to narrow further the time frame of the trend change. Finally, one can act on given timing indications, while taking a predetermined amount of risk. After action had been taken, we can spend as many hours as we like discussing the "whys."

The following is a brief listing of the organizational elements of this book:

1. A brief discussion of history as it relates to metals, as well as the importance of traditionally accepted historical theories (or lack thereof).
2. An introduction to price cycles: their formulations, use, abuse, and advantages, with specific attention focused on metals.
3. Definitions of the various stages within each cycle, with particular emphasis placed on the investment implications of each phase.
4. The use of timing indicators in conjunction with the cycles. Long-term weighted moving averages and chart formations are given particular attention.
5. An explanation of the combined approach using a model portfolio and specific historical examples.
6. Methods of trend forecasting using cycles; the do's and don'ts of forecasting; forecasting versus predicting.
7. Seasonal factors in the metals. An in-depth look at the intrayear factors that have validity in metal trends, including the concepts of "critical month" and "key date."
8. A look at the precious metals themselves, with attention given to strategic use, price spreads, interrelationships, percentage gain, risk, and reward.
9. The ideal structure of a portfolio for the long-term metals investors.
10. Organizational guidelines for precious metals investors; including charts, services, newsletters, brokers, and how to make the best use of them all.

11. Emotion, psychology, and panic—their role in precious metals and
     how to avoid the pitfalls.
12. Summary, forecasts, and suggestions for further readings and re-
     search.

At various points in this book I make suggestions for additional readings.
These suggestions are intended either for those who wish to understand the
given concepts in greater detail and/or for those who wish to pursue a given
topic and require resource information.

In closing, it is important to acquaint you with the necessary caveats that
must accompany any book dealing with investment and money. As you know,
every investment contains inherent risk. In some cases, risk is considerably
greater than in others. In general, however, risk and reward go hand in hand.
The more one seeks to gain on any one investment, the greater is the risk involved. Historically, precious metals have been among the highest percentage
return investment, yet they have also, quite naturally, required the greatest
risk.

I would be remiss were I not to forewarn you about the risks that are a necessary part of metal investment in the precious metals. The degree of risk
varies with the type of investment. There is, of course, considerably more risk
involved in trading futures than in trading mining stocks. Since it is not the primary purpose of this book to acquaint you with the many vehicles for trading
in metals, I will not give you an in-depth analysis of these items. Rather, I
strongly urge the uneducated to become educated. Many reference sources on
precious metals exist, and your local library is probably the best place to begin
your research. Above all, remember that investment and speculation without
risk is not possible (when laws are obeyed).

Finally, the theoretical considerations advanced in this book are still in the
formative stages. They are not presented as perfect, nor should they be taken
as such. Neither my work, nor the cycles on which it is based, will ever be perfectly understood. Therefore, those who wish to implement the theory I present should do so slowly and with sufficient planning. All necessary efforts
should be taken to study my techniques and suggestions prior to implementation. Once implemented, the concepts and methods should be accompanied by
risk-limiting stops and a full knowledge of the inherent risks.

The above should serve as sufficient warning to the experienced, as well as
the uninitiated, investor. The old market adage, "When in doubt—stay out,"
has considerable value in this case. If there is any situation in the market place
that is unclear, whether as a function of my analyses or as a function of intrinsic market developments, your best policy is to stand aside. The caveats I have
presented should be taken seriously. People have a tendency to ignore what
seems redundant, perhaps because they *already* know what is being said. It has
been shown, for example, that many airline passengers ignore the safety guidelines presented at the start of each flight; yet it has also been shown that those
who do listen, regardless of how many times they've heard the instructions before, and that those who take the time to familiarize themselves with an "es-
cape plan," tend to have a greater chance for survival in the event of a mishap.
Investing is, in many respects, the same as air travel. You must plan your exit

as soon as you get on board. You must know how to get out if something goes wrong. It is true that some losses are unavoidable, but it is also true that losses can be minimized through sufficient planning and knowledge.

The last one hundred years have seen many different approaches to price analysis and forecasting. The traditional avenues, which had their roots in economic theory, attempted to determine how the forces of supply and demand balanced at any given point to arrive at a forecast of price trends. Many brilliant economic minds, however, met their sad defeat in the area of price prediction, not only in precious metals and stocks, but in economic trends as well. To determine where prices are headed using a strict econometric approach is a worthwhile and logical goal if one assumes that prices are affected only by economic events. It is quite clear, however, that the psychology of speculation, as well as fear and greed, comprises a major portion of the price trend formula. To seek answers, therefore, without access to total information is unsatisfactory and incomplete.

Efforts to correct this incomplete situation were made as investors, analysts, and traders turned to "technical price analysis." The objective was to work almost exclusively with the various parameters of price, including trading volume, price charts, price chart formations, moving averages, mathematical formulae, and pattern recognition techniques. These methods were more compatible with the scientific direction of the investment arena, and they have come to full fruition with the advent of computer technology.

The pioneers of technical chart analysis, Edwards and McGee, attracted considerable attention, and their classic methods are still used and highly respected today.* Richard Donchian, father of the "moving average system" was also instrumental in bringing price forecasting and trading into the realm of scientific methodology.† Still widely used today, moving average systems and the many variations thereof have added an important dimension of technical analysis and system trading to the storehouse of *analytical tools*.

In addition, many lesser known technical trading systems have surfaced throughout the years. Among these systems are various oscillator methods, point-and-figure charting, pattern recognition systems, and seasonal trading programs. In addition, the proliferation of computer-based systems involving complex mathematical formulations has been responsible for adding literally hundreds of new technical approaches to the trading arena.

---

* R. D. Edwards and J. Magee, *Technical Analysis of Stock Trends* (Springfield, MA: John Magee, 1948).

† Richard D. Donchian, *"Trend-Following Methods in Commodity Price Analysis,"* *Commodity Year Book* (1957), pp. 35–47. Commodity Research Bureau: Jersey City, NJ.

1

The Nature of Cycles

Most individuals who are attracted to the metals futures markets feel that the best way to maximize return on their money is to trade for the short term. Their reasoning is quite logical. "After all," the person argues, "I can make more money trading each turn in the market than I can by staying in for the long pull." On the surface this makes sense! The conclusion, however, presupposes a virtually infallible short-term trading technique that, as experience teaches, is a rare if not totally nonexistent commodity. Although I am not saying that it is impossible for an individual investor to net considerable profit from trading short-term market swings, I am saying that the odds do not favor successful completion of such a task. I have observed, time and time again, individuals who are correct about the trend of a given market, but who, in fact, end up with zero profit or with losses because they did not follow a long-term orientation. I have said many times before, and I will say it again, that short-term trading, or the "hook" as I call it, is not for the average investor. No matter how often I make this point, however, there are still the doubting Thomases who either feel omnipotent or have succumbed to the popular myth that it is indeed possible to "scalp" the markets.

It is possible, of course, to make money trading for the short term. Nevertheless, *most* individuals cannot make the type of time investment necessary to trade effectively during the short term. Many futures investors are professional people who have considerable demands on their time. A physician or attorney who must practice his or her particular skill, for example, cannot leave the operating room or courtroom to call a broker (although some probably do). Short-term trading is a full-time business venture. Consequently, it must be treated as such, and total dedication is necessary, or losses and inconsistency will be the end result. Many techniques have been developed for short-term trading; several will be discussed later in this book. Most, if not all, techniques, however, require constant market monitoring and considerable work. Trading by computer, the new wave in investing, certainly makes many things possible that were not previously practical. Trading by computer also requires consistency, attention, and most of all *time*.

The issue of short-term trading versus long-term trading is easily resolved as a matter of personal preference, practicality, and individual temperament. Regardless of which avenue is selected, the role of cyclic patterns is a force to be reckoned with. The short-term trader knows how important daily and weekly patterns are in the markets, and the long-term trader knows the value of repetitive price history. Either for those who are unaware of these long-standing relationships or for those who are skeptical, I offer the explanation that follows as a brief discourse on cycles, as well as some limited evidence of their existence and behavior. Many texts offer a more thorough analysis.*

You should know, prior to my discussion, that I use the terms "cycles," "patterns," "seasonals," "seasonality," and "repetitive behavior" interchangeably. They all refer to essentially the same type of thing. The key is *repetition*. For my work, anything that is relatively predictable as a function of its repetition or tendency toward repetition is considered cyclical. I am not using the term "cycle" to refer to symmetrical, sine wave types of events. The essence, as I indicated earlier, is repetition over time, not necessarily *symmetry*.

The trading systems developed during the last fifty years have focused primarily on the isolation and determination of short-term to intermediate-term price trends. In addition, a number of trading systems presented to the public focused primarily on the long term. It is, however, a matter of interpetation as to what constitutes long-term trading as opposed to intermediate-term trading. It is the rare individual indeed who can accumulate and hold a position, whether in stocks or futures, for longer than a one-year period. In fact, the odds of holding a position for longer than six months are considerably greater in stocks than in futures market, due to the intrinsic nature of the futures market with its specific expiration dates and months. Many futures contracts, however, have a two- or three-year life span, and longer-term trading is certainly possible.

It has often been said that "the big money is made in the big pull." Investors, traders, and speculators with considerable experience know that to pay attention to the small up-and-down moves within a secular trend can frequently be destructive to the profit picture of a trading program. Not only does short-term trading increase commission costs, it also increases the probability of error and requires considerably more work than does a well-balanced and instituted program of long-term trading. The traditional chart patterns described by Edwards and McGee have considerable merit in long-term trading programs. They can be used effectively to isolate the start of major price trends, and they can also be used to isolate significant tops and bottoms in most

---

* Jacob Bernstein, *The Handbook of Commodity Cycles: A Window on Time* (New York: Wiley, 1982); Edward R. Dewey and O. Mandino, *Cycles: Mysterious Forces that Trigger Events* (New York: Hawthorn Books, 1971); Edward R. Dewey, *Cycles—Selected Writings* (Pittsburgh: Foundation for the Study of Cycles, 1970).

markets. For this purpose, the investor would use either weekly and/or monthly continuation charts, and/or monthly cash average price charts.

In addition to the more traditional techniques (particularly trend-line and chart-formation analysis described above), cyclic analysis, the study of repetitive price patterns, offers a relativey new and promising area of methodology for the investor and trader. The works of Edward R. Dewey and the Foundation for the Study of Cycles have made significant additions to the fund of investment analysis knowledge. It is unfortunate that so few investors and analysts recognize the value of cyclic analysis in their work, despite their knowlege that many events are cyclical and subject to highly accurate trend forecasts, given the existence of these underlying patterns. Nevertheless, computer technology has slowly and steadily increased our ability both to analyze price cycles and to use them as forecasting tools in assisting our selection of investments. Computer technology has facilitated accumulation of large data bases and software libraries, and their use, in turn, has not only validated cyclic analysis, but has refined it as well. Today more and more traders, speculators, investors, farmers, bankers, and business people are becoming aware of cyclic behavior in the marketplace. Many employ cyclic forecasting methods in their work.

Price forecasting, however, is distinctly different from determination of trends. In forecasting a price move, one seeks to anticipate where prices are going, whereas trend following attempts to "ride the coattails of a price move" after it is clear that the move has started. Forecasting and trend following are, therefore, two distinctly different endeavors. This point is underscored because many individuals fail to distinguish a forecast from a reality. Forecasts do not necessarily become realities; following an established trend, however, significantly reduces risk, thereby increasing potential profits.

Drawing from the work of Edward R. Dewey and the Foundation for the Study of Cycles, I began, in 1970, to apply cyclic analysis to the futures market. I was quite impressed with the results and observed that many markets had distinct cyclic tendencies on both a long-term and short-term basis. My first studies were in the copper market where I had access to work done by the Foundation, including its lengthy copper study involving several hundred years' worth of data. In addition, the Foundation offered a study of cotton cycles that clearly demonstrated not only the existence of cycles in this market but their potential profit as well.* The results were staggering, and I was most impressed with both the copper and cotton cyclic studies. My work thereafter moved toward an analysis of shorter-term cyclic events in the futures markets, and I spent considerable time refining my techniques. In 1981, I authored *The Handbook of Commodity Cycles,* which was a definitive exposition of trading techniques in the futures markets using cyclic analysis.

To understand the nature of cycles is both a simple and a complex task. On the surface it would appear that we are in close touch with all of the forces around us that are governed by cyclic laws. The change from night to day and back to night again, fluctuations of the seasons, biological mechanisms, the

---

* Edward R. Dewey, "The 5.91 Year Cycle in Cotton Prices," *Cycles,* October 1954, *5* (8), pp. 227–283.

cycles in chemical reactions, and a host of other events are all related in one form or another to cyclic patterns. Physicists, biologists, and medical researchers have long been aware of cycles and naturally occurring events, yet they have been uncertain, until recently, about how these cyclic events might be used to human benefit. Dewey, however, clearly demonstrated the existence of repetitive patterns in economic data.* The area of economic cycles has received considerable attention particularly through the works of various economists.†

As stated above, cycles, at least on the surface, appear to be simple. The ordinary conception of a cyclic pattern is a move from a low to a high, back to a low again, with a repetition of the process for x number of times. The more times a process is repeated, the more we tend to call it a cycle. Given a sufficiently long history of price repetition, cycles become natural laws. Cyclic events, of course, affect virtually everything experienced by living organisms. This simple view is clearly expressed in the philosophies of Eastern civilization, and it serves as well as the focal point of many world religions. The process of life, death, and rebirth and the afterlife can be viewed as a cyclic event. Religious writings have, for hundreds of years, reiterated the underlying theme of cyclic repetition. On this basis the cycle and its role is reasonably simple to observe, and its understanding requires no further explanation.

It is, however, a considerably more complex task to understand the manner in which cycles function in economic data. Shown in Figures 1.1 through 1.4 are

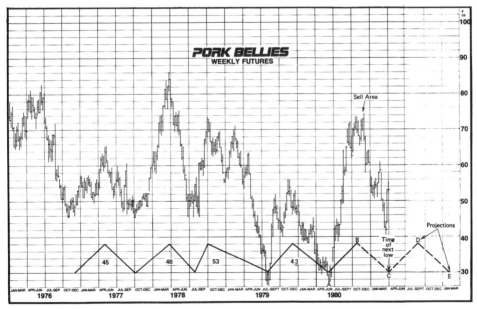

Figure 1.1 The 40–50 week cycle in pork belly futures.
(Reprinted with permission of Commodity Price Charts, 219 Parkade, Cedar Falls, IA 50613.)

* Edward R. Dewey, *Cycles—Selected Writings* (Pittsburgh: Foundation for the Study of Cycles, 1970), Chapter VI.
† See J. A. Schumpeter, *Business Cycles* (New York: McGraw-Hill, 1939).

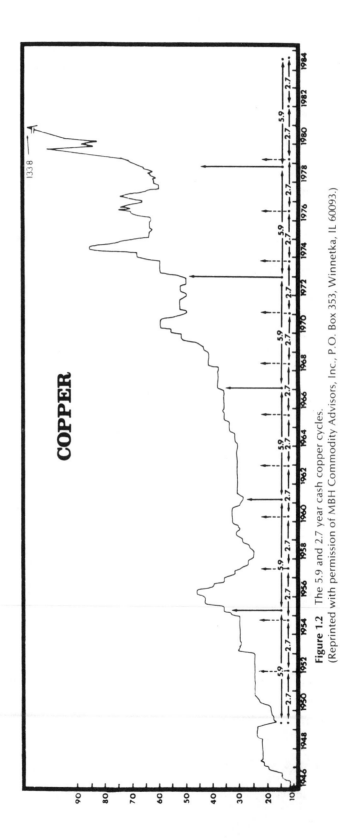

Figure 1.2 The 5.9 and 2.7 year cash copper cycles.
(Reprinted with permission of MBH Commodity Advisors, Inc., P.O. Box 353, Winnetka, IL 60093.)

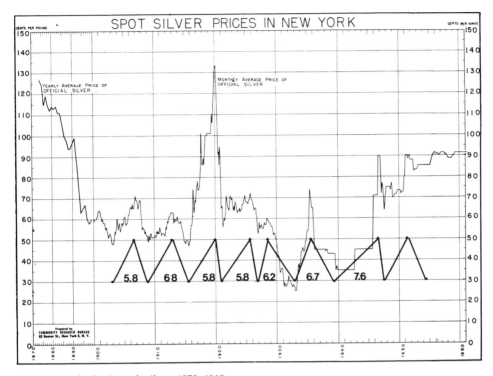

Figure 1.3 Cycles in cash silver, 1870–1960.
(Reprinted with permission of Commodity Research Bureau, 75 Montgomery St., Jersey City, NJ 07302.)

a number of charts that illustrate various cyclic tendencies in a number of different areas. What is shown here is the actual trend of the given variable plotted against an ideal cycle (dashed zigzag line) of the length specified. Cycles are ordinarily measured from top to top and bottom to bottom, although it is possible for a bottom-to-bottom measurement and top-to-top measurement to be given for each cycle. Ordinarily, then, when one refers to the 9.2 year cycle in wheat prices, one is referring to an average cycle length determined for a considerable period of time. Of course, every cycle in wheat prices will not be exactly 9.2 years, rather, the central tendency, or arithmetic mean, will be approximately 9.2 years. Throughout the data base some cycles will be longer and some will be shorter than others. The main consideration is analyzing economic cycles is that to a certain extent they are predictable, and prediction in and of itself implies profit potential. A further and more important consideration in relation to cyclic patterns is the fact that cyclic patterns themselves do not consider news events in their fluctuations. It is an interesting and always uncanny fact that most market-cycle tops are formed on positive news, with most bottoms occurring when the news is the worst. Simply following the news without knowledge of the cycle would lead one to expect a continuation of the trend. The cycle, however, when it is in a topping area, can alert the investor to the fact that the news should not be followed. Literally hundreds of market tops and bottoms can be cited as examples of prices peaking when the news is

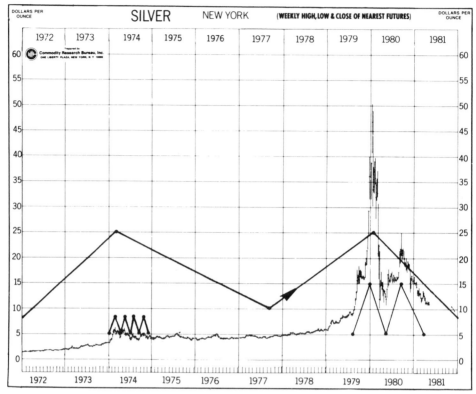

Figure 1.4 Various silver cycles.
(Reprinted with permission of Commodity Research Bureau, 75 Montgomery St., Jersey City, NJ 07302.)

the most promising and bottoming when the news is the most negative. In fact, by following cycles one could in a roundabout way predict when the news would probably be bad and when the news would probably be good. (Please take the time to consider this last, most significant point.)

In addition to cycles that are longer term, there are also many cycles of shorter duration, and I have divided these cycles into several categories:

1. The long-term cycle for our purposes is considered to be any cyclic pattern longer than two years.
2. The intermediate-term cycle is considered to be any cyclic length longer than three months but shorter than two years.
3. The short-term cycle, usually measured in trading days (market days), is any cycle longer than six days but shorter than three months.
4. The ultra short-term cycle is any cycle shorter than six days.

Figures 1.5 through 1.7 show several recent examples of intermediate-term cycles; Figures 1.8 through 1.10 show several recent examples of short-term

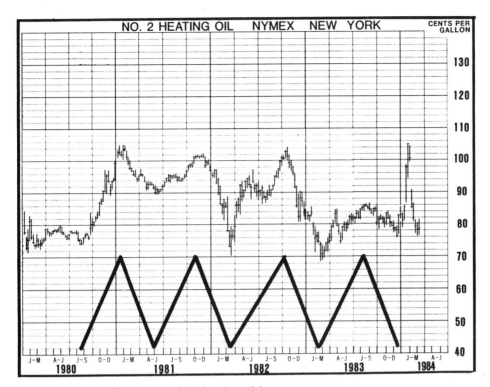

Figure 1.5 Intermediate-term cycle in heating oil futures.
(Reprinted with permission of Commodity Research Bureau, 75 Montgomery St., Jersey City, NJ 07302.)

cycles; and Figures 1.11 through 1.13 show several recent examples of ultra short-term cycles. (Anyone interested in a more detailed explanation of intermediate and short-term cycles should consult my 1981 publication, *The Handbook of Commodity Cycles*, which provides an excellent overview of trading patterns, techniques, and methods I recommend in the use and analysis of intermediate and short-term cycles in the futures markets.)

From your observation of the cycles shown, it should be quite clear that cycles in the marketplace are not necessarily symmetrical. In up-trending markets, tops tend to come late, whereas in down-trending markets, tops tend to come early. The investor who is waiting for cycles to repeat themselves exactly will be sadly disappointed and will probably miss many opportunities to acquire a position either on the long or short side. Figure 1.14 shows the typical bull market patterns in conjunction with the cycles. You will observe that most of the price movement is in the upward direction with weights to the down side comprising progressively less and less movement in magnitude. As a longer-term cyclic peak is approached, the tops come even later, after which the market usually enters into a period of transition and a decline begins. Figure 1.15 shows the bear market cyclic pattern with tops coming early and bottoms coming late. As the market approaches a longer-term bottom, tops become significantly shorter with most of the time being spent in down trend. The market then enters a period of transition and turns higher only to assume its bull mar-

Figure 1.6 Intermediate-term cycle in gold futures.
(Reprinted with permission of Commodity Research Bureau, 75 Montgomery St., Jersey City, NJ 07302.)

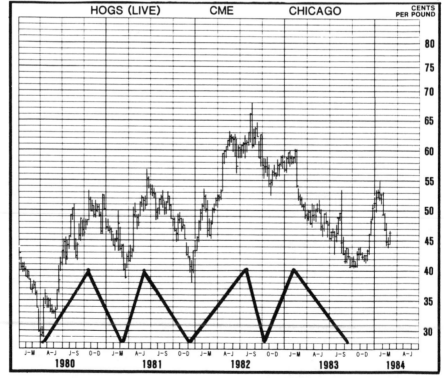

Figure 1.7 Intermediate-term cycle in live hog futures.
(Reprinted with permission of Commodity Research Bureau, 75 Montgomery St., Jersey City, NJ 07302.)

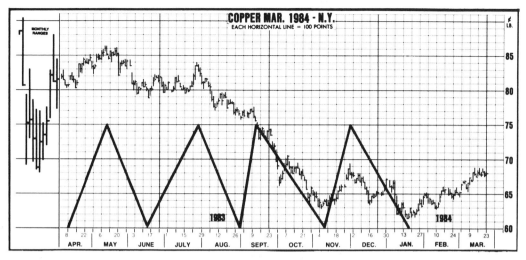

Figure 1.8 Short-term copper cycles.
(Reprinted with permission of Commodity Research Bureau, 75 Montgomery St., Jersey City, NJ 07302.)

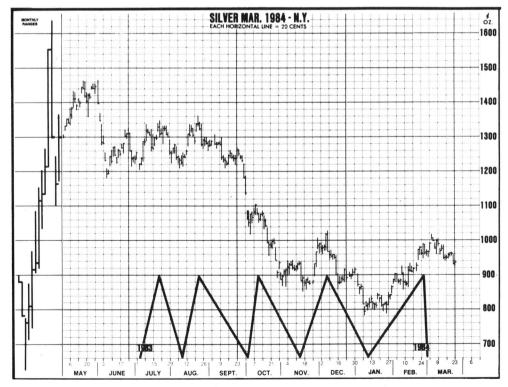

Figure 1.9 Short-term silver cycles.
(Reprinted with permission of Commodity Research Bureau, 75 Montgomery St., Jersey City, NJ 07302.)

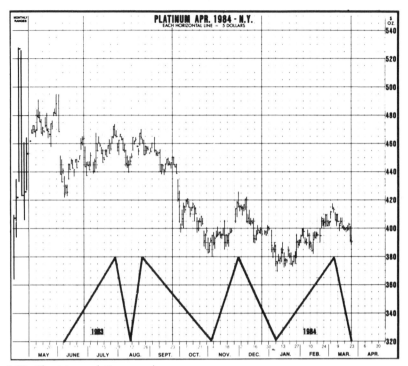

Figure 1.10 Short-term platinum cycles.
(Reprinted with permission of Commodity Research Bureau, 75 Montgomery St., Jersey City, NJ 07302.)

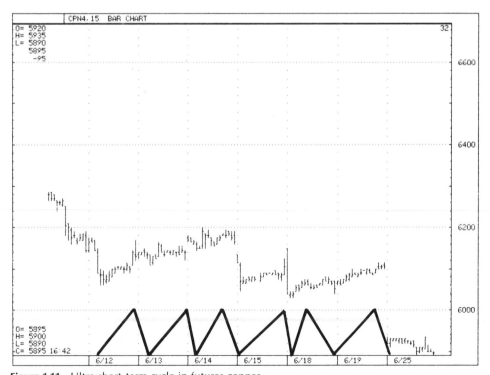

Figure 1.11 Ultra short-term cycle in futures copper.
(Reprinted with permission of Commodity QuoteGraphics, P.O. Box 758, Glenwood Springs, CO 81602.)

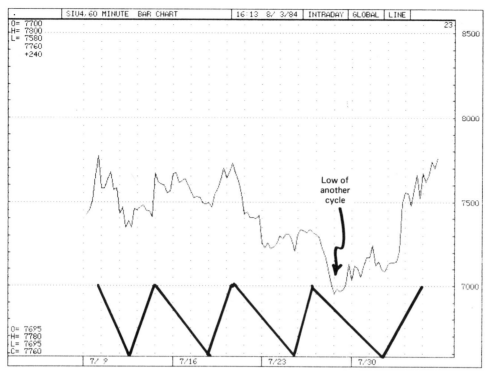

Figure 1.12 Ultra short-term cycle in silver futures.
(Reprinted with permission of Commodity QuoteGraphics, P.O. Box 758, Glenwood Springs, CO 81602.)

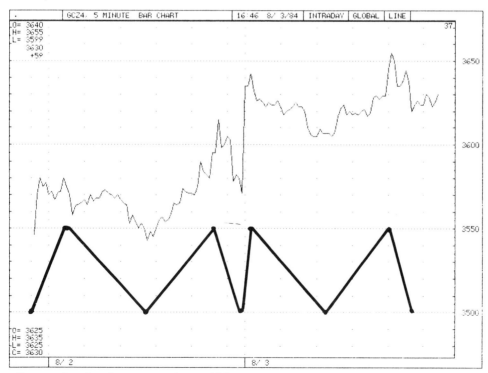

Figure 1.13 Ultra short-term cycle in gold futures.
(Reprinted with permission of Commodity QuoteGraphics, P.O. Box 758, Glenwood Springs, CO 81602.)

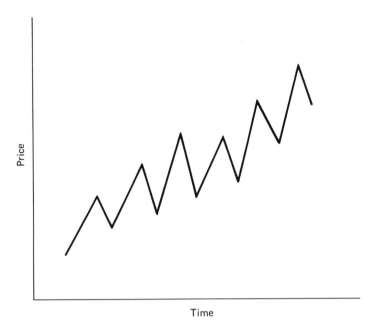

Figure 1.14 Typical bull market cycles pattern.

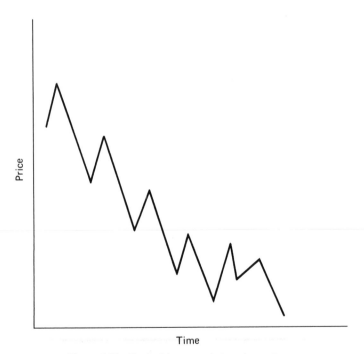

Figure 1.15 Typical bear market cycles pattern.

ket pattern. Figures 1.16, 1.17, and 1.18 illustrate real time examples of bull market patterns, and Figures 1.19, 1.20, and 1.21 illustrate real time examples of bear market patterns. As you can see from the accompanying wave drawings (heavy black lines), the pattern closely resembles the models presented earlier in Figures 1.14 and 1.15.

In summary, then, we can clearly see that cycles are characterized by the following specific factors: (1) repetition; (2) similar average time span between lows and highs during a given period of time; (3) lengthy history of repetition; and (4) bull and bear market charcteristics previously described. There are, in addition, many different ways in which cycles can be used or, for that matter, abused. With some knowlege of what is typical and atypical in cyclic tendencies, however, the investor will usually acquire sufficient knowledge of anomalies in cyclic patterns and will recognize cycles that are tracking according to expectations.

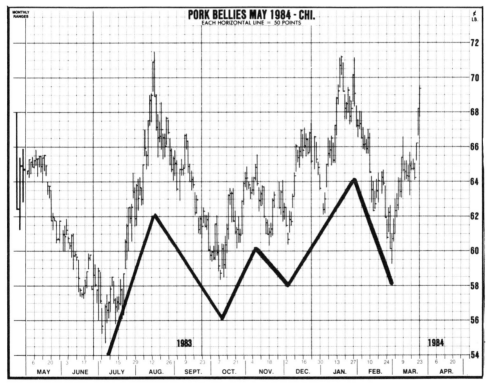

Figure 1.16   Bull market pattern.
(Reprinted with permission of Commodity Research Bureau, 75 Montgomery St., Jersey City, NJ 07302.)

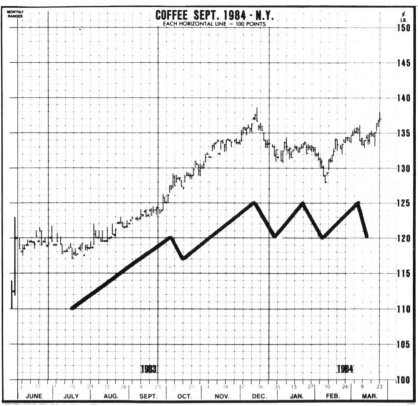

Figure 1.17 Bull market pattern.
(Reprinted with permission of Commodity Research Bureau, 75 Montgomery St., Jersey City, NJ 07302.)

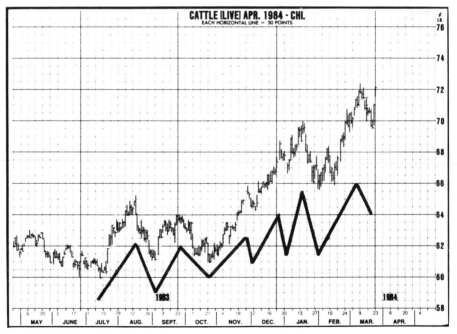

Figure 1.18 Bull market pattern.
(Reprinted with permission of Commodity Research Bureau, 75 Montgomery St., Jersey City, NJ 07302.)

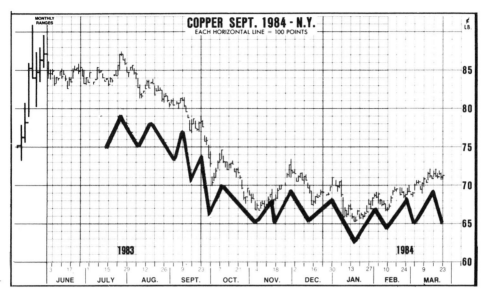

Figure 1.19 Bear market pattern.
(Reprinted with permission of Commodity Research Bureau, 75 Montgomery St., Jersey City, NJ 07302.)

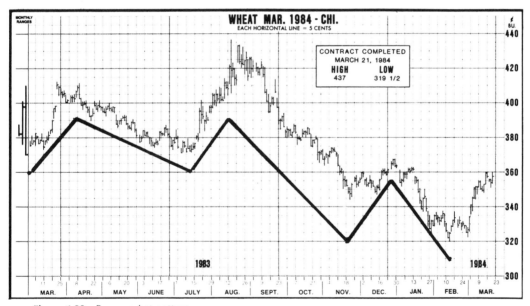

Figure 1.20 Bear market pattern.
(Reprinted with permission of Commodity Research Bureau, 75 Montgomery St., Jersey City, NJ 07302.)

Figure 1.21 Bear market pattern.
(Reprinted with permission of Commodity Research Bureau, 75 Montgomery St., Jersey City, NJ 07302.)

MARKET	LT	HIGH	LOW	TREND	IT	HIGH	LOW	TREND	ST	HIGH	LOW	TREND	PST/HIGH	PST/LOW	COMMENTS
LvCattle	7.2	1979	1983	up	32	04/83	09/83	up	32	01/17	01/02	up		02/10	Half cycle low due now
LvHogs	3.6	1982	1983	up	45	01/83	07/83	up	28	01/17	01/02	up		02/10	Half cycle low due now
PkBellies	3.6	1982	1983	up	45	01/83	07/83	up	28	01/17	01/02	up		2/30	Half cycle low due now
Corn	5.7	1980	1982	down	43	08/83	07/83	down	54	12/27	01/20	up	02/10	02/24	December lows penetrated
Oats	6.0	1981	1983	up	43	01/83	06/83	up	40	12/20	01/20	up	02/10	03/09	ST trend is higher
Soybeans	7.0	1980	1982	up	46	09/83	07/83	up	54	12/27	01/20	up	02/10	02/24	
Soymeal	7.2	1977	1982	up	46	04/83	07/83	down	54	12/27	01/20	up	02/10	02/24	
Soyoil	4.1	1979	1982	up	46	04/83	07/83	down	54	12/27	01/20	up	02/10	02/24	Strongest of complex
Wheat	4.5	1980	1982	up	55	08/83	07/83	down	54	12/28	01/20	up	02/10	03/06	Wheat/corn spread favors wheat
Cotton	5.9	1980	1981	up	43	06/83	09/81	up	58	11/10	01/09	up	02/15	03/20	
HtgOil	---	----	----	up	41	08/83	12/83	up	28	01/20	DUE	up			
Lumber	4.0	1979	1982	up	42	06/83	late	down	36						
Sugar	6.2	1980	1982	late	56	06/83	late	down	56	IT low now being formed					
O.J.	3.1	1982	1981	down	35		02/83	up	60			Avoid short side			
Cocoa	3.7	1978	1982	up	44	06/83	09/83	up	54	Still overbought					Tentative top made 1/4
Coffee	6.7	1977	1981	up	55		02/83	up	55	12/14	01/04	up			
Copper		1980	1982	up	45	05/83		down	38	05/83	DUE	down	12/30		ST and IT lows due
Silver	5.5	1980	1982	up	45	02/83	03/83	down	38	12/30	12/16				
Gold	6.3	1980	1982	up	45	02/83	03/83	down	38	12/30	12/16				
Platinum	5.5	1980	1982	up	40	02/83	03/83	down	38	12/30	12/16				
Palladium	5.5	1980	1982	up	40	02/83	03/83	up	38	12/20	01/09	up			LT bullish
TBills	4.5	1976	1981	up	21	10/83	08/83	down	29	01/13	due				
TBonds	4.5	1976	1981	up	21	05/83	08/83	down	29	01/16	due				
SwFranc	3.0	1980	late	down	41	01/83	08/83	down	52						
DMark	3.0	1980	late	down	41	01/83	08/83	down	52						
BrPound	6.1	1980	late	down	42	01/83	08/83	down	52						
JYen	4.9	1978	1980	down	42	05/83	09/83	up	52	12/30	01/12				
CDollar	5.9	1980	1978	down	21	06/83	08/83	down	28	12/29	01/09				
S&PIndex	4.0	1981	1982	up	23	10/83	due		up	14					
CRBIndex	3.5	1980	1982	up	45	05/83	07/83	up	no	No ST cycle					

Explanatory Notes: Lt=Long Term Cycle length measured in years and fractions. IT=Intermediate Term Cycle length measured in weeks. ST=Short Term Cycle length measured in market days. All cycles are measured low to low. ST cycles are measured in market days not calendar days. Cycle lengths are approximate and subject to change over time. Dates listed are tentative and subject to change when more data becomes available. "---" indicates that our research has not yet revealed any cycle of reliability or that our data base is too limited. Cycles are not necessarily symmetrical. PST/HIGH is our Projected Short High and PST/LOW is our Projected Short Term Low. These projections are not buy or sell recommendations. They will change from week to week as further evaluations are made, and they are included merely as a guide to expectations. No recommendations are made in the above tabular presentations and listed dates, lengths, projections will change as more research is done.

Figure 1.22 Cycle analysis sheet.
(Reprinted with permission of MBH Commodity Advisors, Inc., P.O. Box 353, Winnetka, IL 60093.)

CHARACTERISTIC CYCLE LENGTHS

As I stated earlier, cycles are measured according to time lengths between the lows and/or the highs. Frequently, it is quite simple to find the lows and the highs; on occasion, however, it becomes a more complex task, particularly where other cycle lengths are involved. There can be many different cycle lengths for a given market all operating at the same time. It is possible, for example, that the 5.7 year cycle in silver is in a declining phase, while the 11-month cycle is in a rising phase, and the approximately 38 day cycle is also in a declining phase during a seasonal up trend. This, of course, is a complex situation that causes the individual cycles to become either elongated or shortened. If we had at our disposal all knowledge about the many cycles at work in a given market at any point in time, we could construct an almost perfect forecast of the future trend. Since this is not possible, however, we must be content with the information we have available. I differentiate between a number of short-term, long-term, intermediate, and seasonal cycles in all of the markets. Figure 1.22 contains an example of a summary sheet I use in my weekly work in the futures markets showing the various markets, their cycle lengths, their last lows, their last highs, and their projected lows and highs on the short-term cycles. In addition, other cycles not covered in Figure 1.22 will be discussed in the text that follows. The guidelines in Figure 1.22, however, should be considered when determining, researching, and/or discussing cycle lengths.

2

The Relative Unimportance of History in Precious Metals

During my college days I had a professor who told me that the best place to begin a writing assignment was with the historical background of the given subject. He also told me that the best place to begin the historical coverage was with ancient Greece or, as a good alternative, the Bible. Through the years I started appreciating the value of his suggestions in lengthening the number of pages in any assignment by at least 15%. Except for little known or obscure topics, I began to believe that to give much attention to ancient history constitutes nothing more than space filler. It creates boredom and impresses no one. Unless some heretofore unknown facts, are presented or unless some distinctly new parallels are drawn, I seek to avoid both the reading and writing of history that has already been written and read many times before. The wheel of history has already been invented and reinvented. Why reinvent it once more?

With this in mind I intend to dispense with the history of metals in one fell swooop. Suffice it to say that there are literally hundreds, perhaps thousands, of books, articles, movies, poems, parables, fables, and more, pertaining to gold, silver, and other metals. These books are available in local libraries throughout the world. Gold and silver are favorite topics of the Bible. History books are saturated with metal-related facts, figures, ideas, dates, and so on. I might have increased the size of this book by 15%, perhaps even 25% with a little effort, if I had given the topic more extensive coverage. I have opted, however, to give space to pragmatics rather than to romanticism. There are several wonderful historical tales to be told about precious metals. But after all is said and done, those who know how and when to buy metals, how long to hold them, and how to trade them, will emerge as the victors. In fact, they are probably the ones who donated the money to commission the historical writings about metals.

In summary, here are several key points about precious metals, human-kind, and history:

1. Metals have always served humans as a stable medium of monetary exchange.
2. Metals are the basic form of exchange and virtually all attempts to re-place metals have failed and will likely continue to fail.
3. Metals have intrinsic value resulting from their relative scarcity and beauty.
4. Metals have been a source of financial refuge during times of political and/or economic instability.
5. During recent years the price of precious metals has been exceptionally volatile as world tensions have risen almost exponentially.
6. Metal investments can take many different forms, such as bullion, shares (stocks), gold backed bonds and insurance, options, bullion coins, numismatic and bullion coins combined, mineral rights, and probably a few forms I am not even aware of.
7. Metals will probably continue to serve their historically important roles as outlined above and in countless texts.
8. A close relationship probably exists among petroleum prices, interest rates, currency values, inflation, deflation, budget deficits, economics, and precious metals prices.
9. The ultimate question underlying all precious metals investments is *timing*. Regardless of what importance one attributes to metals, the key question has always been and will always be "When to buy and sell?"

It is to this last question that the greatest attention must be given. Recognizing the relative importance of this topic, I have focused this book on the *timing* issue. Though history is important, it is something we can learn at our leisure.

In conclusion, then, and in defense of my decision to gloss over the history of metals, I urge you to consider seriously the extreme importance of the timing issue. In the area of investments there have been literally millions of fortunes lost or not acquired as a function of poor timing. We all know people who were either ahead of their time or behind their time. To be ahead of one's time is a greater virtue in the area of speculation and investment than it is to be behind the time. Both, however, can lead to the same frustration and financial ruin. To be in the right place and to be there at the right time is the ultimate combina-tion. The study of history can contribute only minimally to successful timing. Whereas history does indeed repeat itself, it does not always do so in precisely the same fashion. Nor does it do so at precisely the same time. The historical summary of metals given earlier in this brief chapter intentionally left out what I consider to be *the major point* regarding the history of metals. I did so in order to make its impact greater. The point is a simple one on the surface, but it is exceptionally complex in its ramifications. *Precious metals prices have moved in cycles.* These cycles, though not symmetrical, have had a good his-tory of reliability, with lows and highs of major price moves falling within reasonably close time frames. Is it possible, therefore, that to know cycles is to know history? There is an old expression among professional poker players that "if you know poker you know people." What this means is that by knowing the *rules,* both written and unwritten, of poker, you know how people will react in a variety of situations. In effect, this is a variation on the "black box theory," which I will discuss shortly. Here is what I am saying about cycles: *If you know cycles, then you know history.* I have always maintained that cycles will most often tell you that *something* important will happen. They will not always tell you exactly *what* it is that will happen. With a little knowledge of history and current events, however, you can fairly well determine exactly *what* it is that is *likely* to happen. You can determine in a reasonably educated way *what* the news will be that will make prices move. But by knowing the cycle you will probably know in advance that there will be some news. The value of this knowledge is so immense that it is often inestimable to the investor.

In another publication I made the following observations about history and cycles:

> The history of mankind is the history of cycles. Since the beginning of recorded time civilizations have grown, matured, and disappeared leaving only artifacts as remembrances of their existence. Time and time again the process of birth, growth, maturity and death has woven its finality into the fiber of man's being. Indeed cycles are all around us—the passing of night into day, the sunset and a return to night, only to be followed once more by day; the rise and fall of ocean tides; planetary movement; the arrival and departure of seasons—to name but a few.
>
> Even religion speaks of a cycle-like process. When the physical body dies it passes to another state and is, in effect, reborn. The teachings of Buddhism, Shinto, and Eckankar can be viewed from a cyclical standpoint. Although the form of life may change, the process is endless and repetitive. "The thing that hath been, it is that which shall be; and that which is done is that which shall be done: and there is no new thing under the sun" (Ecclesiastes 1.9). The history of mankind is the history of cycles. To understand cycles is to understand life.
>
> Our daily lives are ever influenced by the limitations of our environment. And our environment is, in turn, regulated by repetitive patterns such as light/dark, warm/cold, and wet/dry. Within these constraints our social, psychological, and economic systems operate, seemingly in a random dance of events. Once we gain awareness of the world around us we realize in amazement how the patterns of our lives repeat themselves, time and time again. And so it is in the world of commodities. Contemporary science is clearly aware of biological clocks within the animal kingdom but somehow hesitant to accept their existence in the social and economic worlds. Indeed, considerable study is necessary to isolate the role of cycles from random events. The academic pursuit of cycles has not yet attained a role of prominence in the scientific community, since it is an idea that is ahead of its time. Simple as cycles may be to comprehend, man may not yet be prepared to comprehend and appreciate the role of cyclical science in all phases of life.*

* Jacob Bernstein, *Commodities Now Through 1984* (Winnetka, IL: MBH, 1982). p. 4.

THE "BLACK BOX" THEORY

My efforts toward pragmatism and academic parsimony, in both the pursuit of investment and other areas, have brought me to a firm belief in the "black box theory" of behavior. In science the "law of parsimony" simply states that "if a 10 word explanation serves to fully describe a situation, why use 100 words?" This is the direction in which I have moved, and it is also the direction in which I suggest all investors move. The days of long-winded academicism are gone. They have been replaced with pragmatism, computer technology, productivity, and specificity. It is no longer necessary to understand a situation in order to describe the situation. The *why* of things is gradually being replaced with the *how* of things. The use of multivariate and univariate statistical methods (i.e., Box-Jenkins and regression analyses) allows a given curve to be expressed as a formula that will predict future values of the curve. These future values are not predicted with the assistance of historical events. Rather, they are predicted as a function of statistical history. It is the history of prices we want to know and not necessarily the history of events that is significant.

Now enters the "black box." Humor me for a while as I set the stage for my theory. Once explained I will not burden you with it for the rest of this book. I believe, however, it is an important philosophical issue for the investor, particularly as it pertains to history, fundamentals, economics, investment methods, and prices. Let us assume that the market and every single thing that makes it move are contained in a box. I call it a "black box" to add to the dramatics and mystery surrounding the box. There are many things within the market black box. In fact, there are so many things inside the box that we cannot possibly know all of them. Nor can we know all the ways in which they interact. If, for example, there are 50 major variables that affect prices, each having its own ranking in terms of importance, there may be 50 factorial combinations (expressed mathematically as 50!, which means $50 \times 49 \times 48 \times 47 \times \ldots .3 \times 2 \times 1$). That's a huge number of combinations. I would venture to say that there are considerably more than 50 variables. I believe it is a safe assumption that we will *never* know precisely how all of these variables interact. Nor will we ever know exactly how important each variable really is. I submit, therefore, that to try and figure out what is inside the "black box" is an exercise in futility. There is a much better way to go about things.

What I suggest is the same approach that has been used by behavioral psychologists. Their approach was derived from physics and chemistry. While one branch of science tries to figure out *why* things work, another branch of science, the empirical branch, examines only inputs and outputs. Note the model depicted in Figure 2.1. What it shows is the "black box," a variety of inputs, and a variety of outputs. By studying the inputs and outputs we can determine how they are related. In other words, by knowing what types of things go into the box we can learn what will come out.

The essence of the black box idea is that it bypasses the box itself, while allowing you to reach several valid conclusions about the functioning of the box. Then, after the inputs and output patterns or relationships have been determined, the "guts" of the box can be determined. But by then the "guts" of

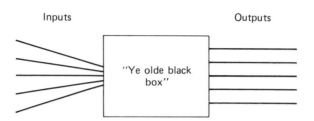

Figure 2.1   Idealized black box showing inputs and outputs.

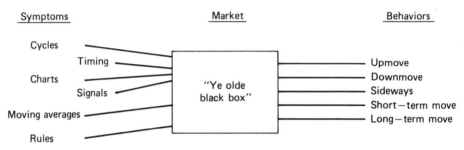

Figure 2.2   The market analysis paradigm — black box theme variation.

the black box are a moot point. They do, however, make good fireplace conversation on cold winter nights. What I am saying in this respect is that one can determine what will occur based merely on an understanding of what goes into a given "black box." In this case, the "black box" is the market. We know that certain things happen when the market is ready to go higher, and we know that certain things happen when the market is ready to go lower. By studying the technical conditions that are part and parcel of the "inputs," we can tell what the market will do (outputs.) The analogy is not a strict one. In essence, what we are doing is determining the *symptomatology* of a market in order to make a *diagnostic* decision about the health of the market. A medical doctor examines given symptoms and reaches a diagnosis regarding the health of the patient. A market technician examines the symptoms of the marketplace and determines the health of the market. There is no need to study history other than how it relates to the *history of the symptoms and their past reliability.*

I hope that my efforts at explaining to you the relative unimportance of history have been productive. Perhaps you are an individual who can benefit from the study of historical events in the marketplace. As I explained previously, however, the importance of timing cannot be overestimated and timing has virtually nothing to do with history. If we assume that cylces are the key to detecting price change, and if we further assume that technical analysis is the only important aspect of determining precise entry and exit, then we have no need to study history. I suggest you examine Figure 2.2, since it is the paradigm of my technical approach in this book. I further suggest that you attempt to clear your mind of all market facts you have previously learned if these facts are in any way related to history. History will be replaced with cycles, and your "gut" reactions to history and current events will be replaced by objective timing indicators.

3

Anatomy of a Cycle

Cyclic trends have existed for literally thousands of years. Edward R. Dewey, frequently called the "Father of Cycles," was the first individual to popularize the notion that economic trends, securities, and commodity prices move in predictable, fairly regular cyclic patterns. This does not imply that all cycles are symmetrical, nor does it imply that cycles are not subject to considerable variation. Nevertheless, the concept of cyclic price movement is most important. This topic has been discussed and explained earlier, and there are many examples of cyclic price patterns in the metals and precious metals.

Perhaps the greatest single feature of the price cycle is its divisibility into several specific phases: each phase has its own characteristic price behavior; and each phase can be fairly readily identified on price charts. Knowing the different cyclic phases will, therefore, enable the investor to determine where the cycle stands and thus to make appropriate investment decisions. Furthermore, each cyclic phase has its own behavioral characteristic of both price and fundamentals; this further assists the investor in making appropriate investment decisions both on the long side and short side. Let it be said at the outset that the cycle itself does not seek to predict but rather to follow trend. Although there is a rather subtle distinction in terms of definition, the distinction between trend following and forecasting is indeed an important one.

Forecasting in and of itself is both at once a difficult and risky undertaking. Ordinarily, the individual who forecasts attempts to predict price rather than trend. This is perhaps where the first error is committed. It is far easier to forecast trend than it is to forecast price. The cycle allows one to forecast trend, but in and of itself trend forecasting can also be a dangerous and costly undertaking. In effect, it is difficult for Western people to divorce themselves from the notion that "things" *must* go in a particular direction. We have been raised with the underlying belief that life *must* follow a predetermined course and

that certain things *must* occur, milestones *must* be followed, and socially acceptable goals *must* be attained. Few of us believe that life must follow whichever course it takes. Certainly we have no control over the future, nor do we
have control over the future of the markest (or, for that matter, the futures
market). Consequently, to anticipate is not necessarily a constructive attitude
in the marketplace. The most appropriate attitude is simply to follow the market, since to follow the market is an admission that you do not know where it is
going, but that you want to go wherever it takes you. "So what," you might ask,
"do I need the cycle for?" The answer is simple. The cycle will allow you to determine the direction of the market and the manner in which it should be entered.

There are essentially 7 phases of the cycle:

1. The bottoming phase during which cycles establish a low.
2. The accumulation phase, during which knowledgeable investors begin
   to accumulate positions.
3. The strong growth phase, during which prices accelerate sharply.
4. The topping phase, during which prices peak out and begin to give indications that lower prices are inevitable.
5. The decline phase, during which prices begin their initial decline.
6. The recovery phase, the period of brief recovery after initial reaction to
   the down side.
7. The final down wave, during which prices move down sharply prior to
   establishing their low and returning to phase one of the cycle.

The present discussion will make extensive use of Figure 3.1, which is a paradigm of the ideal cyclic phasing.

PHASE 1: THE BOTTOMING PHASE

During this portion, the cycle prices are attempting to form a low after
having been down for a considerable period of time as part of the previous
downward cycle. Typically, the bottoming phase can take either of two distinct
forms. The first form is characterized a *panic liquidation,* during which prices
fall sharply and consistently during a brief period of time, therby resulting in
panic selling by the public and investors and giving rise to an oversold condition and a subsequent bull market. Typically, the news backdrop of the bottoming phase is characterized by bearish investor sentiment, extremely
negative fundamentals, a lack of interest among professionals, and no fundamental reason for a change in trend. Climax-type bottom ordinarily witnesses
most of these news developments happening within a relatively brief period of
time. On the other hand, the second type of bottom, or what I call an extended
bottom, tends to see such news occur throughout several months or perhaps
during a period of time lasting as long as one year in the longer-term cycle. In
general, the price range is characterized by narrow movement during the base

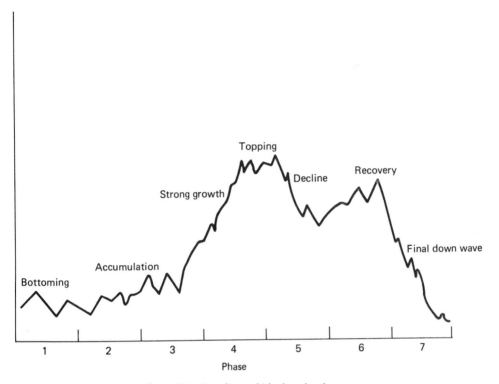

Figure 3.1   Paradigm of ideal cycle phases.

or extended bottoming period such as is characterized in Figures 3.2, 3.3, and 3.4. "Climax" bottoms look similar to those shown in Figures 3.5, 3.6, and 3.7. In terms of technical price characteristics that confirm a low of the cycle, a number of signals can be used to confirm the low. These will be discussed in Chapter 5. The essence of this discussion is merely to provide an overview of the various cyclic phases giving characteristics of each that relate to real market conditions and indicators that the average investor can readily observe and understand.

PHASE 2: ACCUMULATION

During this phase informed investors (otherwise known as insiders) begin strong accumulation in the various markets. It is difficult to ascertain the exact reasons for their accumulation; however, it is not, in fact, necessary to know why insiders buy. Perhaps the greatest reason is that of relative value and price. Typically, informed investors buy low and sell high. After prices have dropped considerably and for a lengthy period of time, forming the base, the attention of well-seasoned investors is drawn to these markets. Furthermore, after some study and analysis of trends, relative value, and economic conditions, they can make decisions regarding market entry and act accordingly.

Figure 3.2 Extended bottom formation in gold futures.
(Reprinted with permission of Commodity Research Bureau, 75 Montgomery St., Jersey City, NJ 07302.)

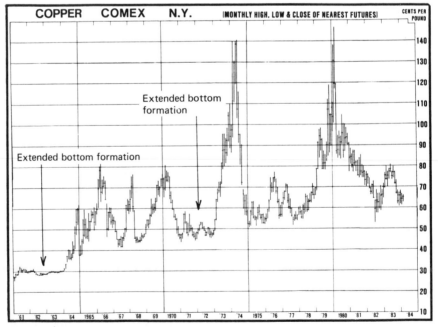

Figure 3.3 Extended bottom formation in copper futures.
(Reprinted with permission of Commodity Research Bureau, 75 Montgomery St., Jersey City, NJ 07302.)

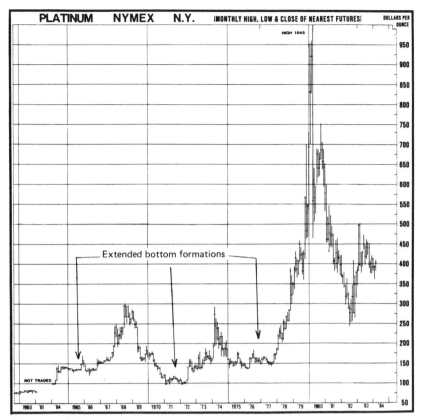

Figure 3.4 Extended bottom formations in platinum futures.
(Reprinted with permission of Commodity Research Bureau, 75 Montgomery St., Jersey City, NJ 07302.)

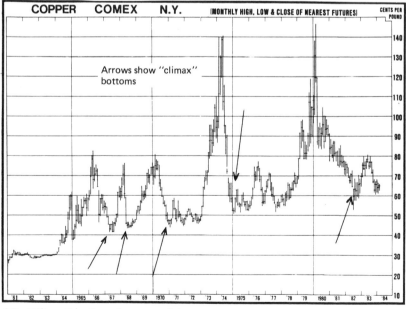

Figure 3.5 "Climax" bottoms in copper futures.
(Reprinted with permission of Commodity Research Bureau, 75 Montgomery St., Jersey City, NJ 07302.)

Figure 3.6 "Climax" bottoms in gold futures.
(Reprinted with permission of Commodity Research Bureau, 75 Montgomery St., Jersey City, NJ 07302.)

Figure 3.7 "Climax" bottoms in platinum futures.
(Reprinted with permission of Commodity Research Bureau, 75 Montgomery St., Jersey City, NJ 07302.)

Their accumulation buying is primarily for the long term, and they are willing to add to positions during the bottoming phase and well into the accumulation phase. Most of their buying, however, is restricted to the accumulation phase during which prices are not accelerating upward at a high rate. Figures 3.8, 3.9, and 3.10 show typical chart patterns during the accumulation phase, and Figures 3.11, 3.12, and 3.13 show several technical indications (to be discussed in Chapter 3) that correlate with the transition from bottoming phase to accumulation phase.

Characteristically, the accumulation phase is marked by specific developments, technically, fundamentally, and behaviorally. The news backdrop still tends to be rather neutral, although some early "bulls" invent good reasons for being on the long side of the market. In general, however, public and professional sentiment are still relatively negative for the longer term, with memories of the previous decline still fresh in the minds of analysts. It is during this relatively neutral to negative environment that insiders continue their accumulations, and negative news developments are also used as opportunities to add to the long-range positions. Fundamentally, this situation is not seriously detrimental. There is, however, no apparent reason for buying the given market and, in fact, reasonable economic explanations can be advanced in opposition to the bullish case. Technically, there are specific developments as well. (These will be discussed later).

Figure 3.8 Accumulation phase (arrows) prior to bull move.
(Reprinted with permission of Commodity Research Bureau, 75 Montgomery St., Jersey City, NJ 07302.)

Figure 3.9 Accumulation phase (arrows) prior to bull move.
(Reprinted with permission of Commodity Research Bureau, 75 Montgomery St., Jersey City, NJ 07302.)

Figure 3.10 Accumulation phase (arrows) prior to bull move.
(Reprinted with permission of Commodity Research Bureau, 75 Montgomery St., Jersey City, NJ 07302.)

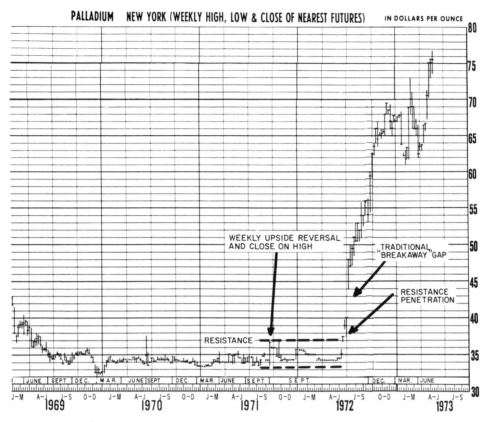

Figure 3.11 A closer look at an accumulation phase in palladium (See Fig. 3.8) showing technical indicators.
(Reprinted with permission of Commodity Research Bureau, 75 Montgomery St., Jersey City, NJ 07302.)

PHASE 3: STRONG GROWTH PHASE

The accumulation phase is typically followed by the phase of strong growth. It is during this time that prices accelerate rather sharply, and it is also during this time that the public first expresses its awareness that a bull market exists. Those who buy early during this strong growth phase will fare well profit-wise provided they can exit the market at or close to the top. Professionals are relatively small buyers during this time and typically think ahead looking for a place to sell out their positions to a ready, willing, and able buying public. Figures 3.14, 3.15, and 3.16 illustrate metal markets in strong growth phases showing the upward acceleration of price as well as the angular acceleration of the market.

Characteristically, the strong growth phase also contains specific elements that help identify it. Fundamentally, the news has turned bullish and, in fact, an extremely good case can be made for sustained up movement in price. Volume of trading and open interest in futures contracts increase, and public awareness of the bull market rises to extemely high levels. Technical chart patterns attract a great deal of attention, and prices continue to gain upward

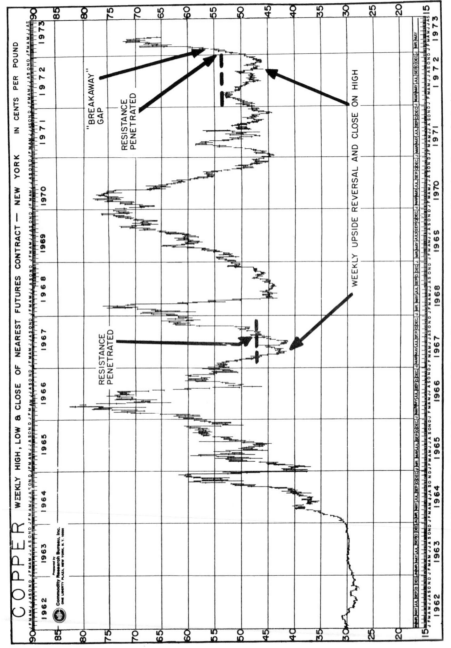

Figure 3.12 A closer look at accumulation bottoms in copper (See Fig. 3.9) showing technical in-dicators.
(Reprinted with permission of Commodity Research Bureau, 75 Montgomery St., Jersey City, NJ 07302.)

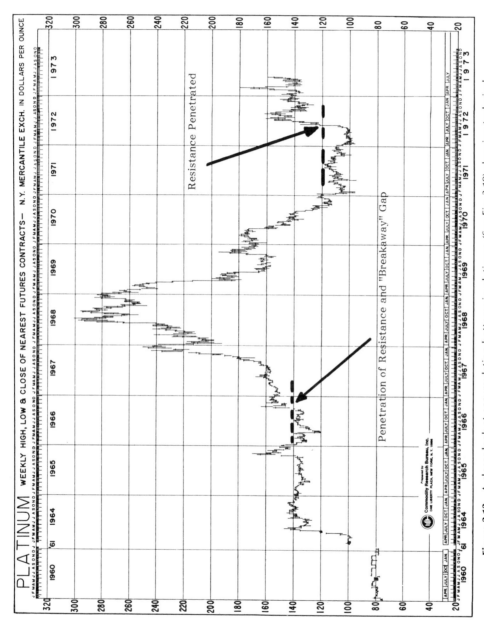

Figure 3.13 A closer look at accumulation bottoms in platinum (See Fig. 3.10) showing technical indicators.
(Reprinted with permission of Commodity Research Bureau, 75 Montgomery St., Jersey City, NJ 07302.)

39

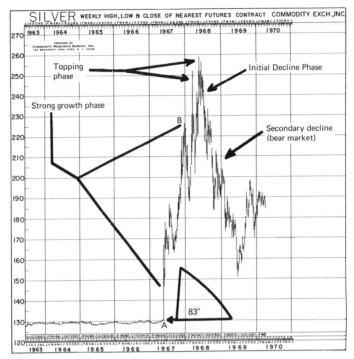

Figure 3.14 Various cyclic phases and angular acceleration of 1967–1968 bull market in silver. (Reprinted with permission of Commodity Research Bureau, 75 Montgomery St., Jersey City, NJ 07302.)

momentum reaching extremely high levels. The news backdrop is, of course, quite positive, and firms specializing in all types of precious metal investments begin heavy advertising campaigns, particularly in the financial press. Another correlate of the strong growth phase is daily price range in the futures markets. In most bull markets, price range increases, along with margin requirements imposed by brokerage firms and futures exchanges. An examination of Figure 3.14 clearly shows price range prior to bull market and price range during strong growth phase. As you can see, there is a marked increase in price movement.

PHASE 4: TOPPING PHASE

Much has been written about the history of markets and the manner in which prices may be predicted. Little, however, has been written about the manner in which markets top and bottom. Major tops in the metal markets are characterized by extreme buying hysteria, large trading volume, significant up movement in prices, and extreme bullishness. Such marked tops are ordinarily characterized by extremely large upward velocity of prices as well as large angular movements. It is not uncommon for the tail end of a major bull market to have an upward slope approaching 90 degrees as the limit. Figures 3.14, 3.15,

Figure 3.15 Strong growth phase and angular acceleration of three different bull markets in platinum.
(Reprinted with permission of Commodity Research Bureau, 75 Montgomery St., Jersey City, NJ
07302.)

and 3.16 illustrate bull market tops shown with the corresponding angular velocity.

There are many things that the long-term investor must do as prices enter
their cyclic peak. (These actions are discussed more fully in Chapter 8.) Suffice
it to say that markets do not spend a great deal of time peaking, and there is,
therefore, limited time during which to act in liquidating a long-range position.
Timing is crucial and a specific technique must be followed in taking profits on
positions previously established during the accumulation and bottoming
phases. Market tops are emotional, seemingly justified purchases based on
fundamentals are common, and the consensus of experts, as well as the public,
is unfailingly bullish with few signs of a top being evident to most investors
when the market is peaking.

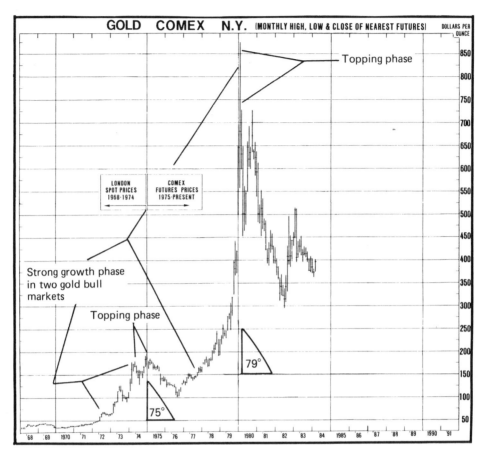

Figure 3.16   Strong growth phase and angular acceleration of two gold bull markets.
(Reprinted with permission of Commodity Research Bureau, 75 Montgomery St., Jersey City, NJ 07302.)

PHASE 5: DECLINE PHASE

The first indication that a bull market is ending is usually seen in an initially sharp decline from record high levels. The decline can be as much as 20% of price within a matter of days. Typically, such a reaction after an extremely bullish move is seen by the public and experts as a buying opportunity, and few believe that the initial decline phase marks a significant top in the formative process. The initial decline, however, is a warning sign that things with the bull market are not right; thus, the long-term investor following the strategy proposed here will be alerted to this technical development and should take appropriate action when the time is right.

In terms of longevity, the initial decline phase is particularly brief and in some cases totally absent. Few bull markets, however, peak without an initial decline phase preceding a secondary test of the top. Figures 3.17, 3.18, and 3.19 show how the initial decline phase appears in reality and what ordinarily transpires subsequent to the initial decline. In technical terminology, the initial de-

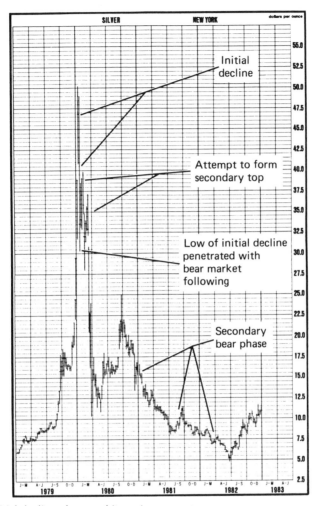

Figure 3.17　Initial decline phase and its various aspects.
(Reprinted with permission of Commodity Research Bureau, 75 Montgomery St., Jersey City, NJ 07302.)

cline is usually followed by a secondary top, and when the low of the initial decline has been penetrated, a double top is said to have been confirmed. In practice, few secondary tops penetrate their previous peak, or do so only briefly. Since the initial decline phase and its subsequent test of the top is a highly emotional period for investors, it is always best for long-term trades to be totally out of the market at this time to minimize the likelihood of investment error.

It has been said that "market tops and bottoms are made by wise men and fools"; this saying is particularly relevant in discussing the secondary peak and initial decline. We can assume, therefore, that to participate in the market during the formation of major tops and bottoms is a foolish undertaking. I assume that since you purchased this book you are not a fool; consequently, I counsel you not to act like one.

In Chapter 4 I will provide you with the tools to help you avoid participation during this stage of the market or, at the very least, to enable you to recognize that the best action to take during this phase is action that is contrary to popular thinking. As you know, of course, I favor contrary actions at most turning points in the markets since contrary action is often correct at major market turns. (Many specifics that technically should be evaluated and considered in identifying this market stage will be discussed in detail in Chapter 4.) Suffice it to say that most investors who succeed do so by avoiding the company of fools, but in so doing they are not necessarily wise men.

The initial decline phase and its secondary subsequent recovery and test of the highs characterize not only precious metals markets and copper, but in addition virtually every other market in existence, whether stocks, bonds, futures, or options. In fact, the initial sharp decline and secondary recovery are likely correlates of all natural events, including human relationships. Technically speaking, the *"M"* top best characterizes the general characteristics of the ini-

Figure 3.18 Initial decline phase and its various aspects.
(Reprinted with permission of Commodity Research Bureau, 75 Montgomery St., Jersey City, NJ 07302.)

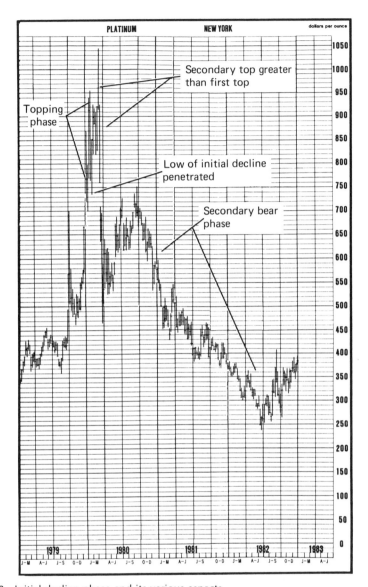

Figure 3.19 Initial decline phase and its various aspects.
(Reprinted with permission of Commodity Research Bureau, 75 Montgomery St., Jersey City, NJ 07302.)

tial decline and secondary recovery stage. Figures 3.20 and 3.21 show two such tops.

PHASES 6 AND 7: THE RECOVERY PHASE AND THE FINAL DOWNWAVE

After an unsuccessful secondary attempt to penetrate the top, prices enter an extended period of decline during which they lose more quickly than they

Figure 3.20 "M" top in platinum futures.
(Reprinted with permission of Commodity Research Bureau, 75 Montgomery St., Jersey City, NJ 07302.)

had gained during the growth phase. Characteristically, bear markets decline much faster than bull markets rise. It is, therefore, possible for a bear maket to erase in several months what has taken several years to build. It is perhaps the forces of gravity at work, but more likely the persistent liquidation that causes bear markets to continue with such force. Figures 3.14, 3.17, 3.18, and 3.19 show recent bear market phases in the metals and the general tendency of the secondary bearish phase. As stated previously, the bear markets tend to result in prices declining at a faster pace than prices rise in a bull market. There is, therefore, less time to act in a bear market, and those who have not liquidated positions in advance of the decline are in a particularly bad position. Perhaps the most dangerous thing to do if you are holding a long position in a bear market is to "wait for a rally." Characteristically, the rallies will never be long enough or large enough for you to take appropriate action, and you may still find yourself holding the position when the market bottoms. The tendency at the bottom, of course, will be to liquidate the position when pain has reached its maximum. The long-term investor who is not inclined to sell short in the futures market is usually not trading at this point in time. His or her position should have been closed out well in advance of the secondary decline phase and a casual wait-and-see attitude can be maintained during the drop. Technically and behaviorally, many aspects characterize the deline phase; in addition, specific actions can be taken by the more aggressive speculator. (These actions will be discussed in Chapter 8.)

The secondary decline phase, of course, has its interspersed rallies, but these usually last for only brief periods of time and constitute nothing more than mere selling opportunities. In the cold light of day, objectivity is easily attainable. In the heat of battle, however, most investors lose sight of the fact that markets do indeed move in waves and do indeed have specific personality traits as well as specific cyclic phases. The information and general explanations provided in this chapter will alert you to what can occur and will describe appropriate actions that might be taken. The more specific symptomatology accompanying each cyclic phase will, as promised, be discussed later. The concept or essence of this chapter is merely to acquaint you with the paradigm providing a general orientation within which prices can be seen. Perspective is an important virtue in the market, and my focus on macro versus micro has been designed to undo the erroneous assumptions that pervade the thoughts of most investors in the 1980s. As indicated at the outset of this book, few people are willing to admit that they believe in long-term investments, although they cannot for various reasons carry their beliefs to behavioral fruition. Perhaps by

Figure 3.21   "M" top in copper futures.
(Reprinted with permission of Commodity Research Bureau, 75 Montgomery St., Jersey City, NJ 07302.)

understanding the repetitive nature of cyclic events and their component phases, the investor will be prompted to take action consistent with his or her beliefs. Not that I am not discounting the possibility of short-term profits; I am merely discounting the probability of short-term profits for the average investor, since the average investor lacks the necessary emotional and financial control.

As a review of the material just presented, please note the following major points relative to long-term cyclic patterns in metals (and most other markets):

1. Chart patterns tend to be similar from one cycle to the next, frequently exhibiting relatively similar characteristics and symptoms.
2. Several different phases identify each cycle, and each phase can be characterized by its price behavior, its human/emotional correlates, its news backdrop, and last but not least its specific timing indicators.
3. Historical chart patterns readily fall into several different categories as previously mentioned and illustrated. Not all markets, however, exhibit all the characteristics mentioned. The various stages mentioned can be either elongated or abbreviated. History in the marketplace, therefore, may repeat itself, *but not in the same way every time.*
4. In addition to the cyclic phases, there are also individual timing patterns, angular characteristics, top and bottom formations, chart gaps, resistance and support points, reversal signals, moving averages, and other indicators that help identify a market phase and/or market turn. These aspects will be discussed in considerable detail in the next chapter.

4

Identifying Cycles in Metals

In Chapter 1 I indicated the importance of cyclic price tendencies in all commodity and stock markets. I also noted that certain cyclic lengths were unique to the precious metals and copper. Specifically, cycles of five–six years, 9–14 months, 9 years, and 54 years seem to be prevalent in copper and precious metals. Given the fact that cycles are not perfect, as well as the fact that cyclic peaks and troughs do not always occur at the precise midpoint of the cycle, many people have questioned the validity of cyclic patterns as a tool for long and short-term investing. To further the current theoretical work on cyclic investing, let us first examine the history of price cycles in copper and silver. These two markets have been chosen due to their lengthy history. The price of gold was fixed in the United States for many years, which, of course, limited fluctuations of this market throughout the world. Silver prices, however, were free to fluctuate; consequently, we were able to observe the cyclic patterns unhampered by government decree or dictum. Copper prices have also had a lengthy history and, indeed, the Foundation for the Study of Cycles has statistics dating back to the 1700s as part of its data bank on the cyclic analysis of copper. For the present discussion, however, only the last 80 years (approximately 13 cycles) will be covered. If it can be adequately demonstrated that a 5–6 year rhythm has existed in copper and silver prices for the last 80 years, the reader will be more receptive to the concept of cyclic investing and will, therefore, find the present work most enlightening and perhaps profitable. Throughout the discussion that follows, remember the cyclic phases that were previously discussed and their relative importance in the overall strategy of cyclic investing. In so doing, you will find it possible to apply the concept and descriptions of cyclic phases discussed in the previous chapters. Thus, you will obtain further practice and insight into market personality and behavior. As the various cycles are discussed in this chapter, I will, occasionally, note some of the cyclic phases to verify and clarify your understanding.

First we will look at the overall picture. Figure 4.1 shows the monthly cash average price of silver since the early 1900s. A cursory examination of this chart will probably result in no dramatic conclusion about cycles in silver prices. From 1900 through the early 1970s, for example, the price of silver did not undergo a great deal of fluctuation. After 1970, however, and well into the 1980s silver prices have moved in a large trading range. In fact, the price action during the 1970s and 1980s makes the previous six decades look infinitesimal by comparison. Any cycles that would appear in the 1900s through 1970s data would be obscured, therefore, when compared to the post-1970s data. The first step, therefore, is to examine the portion of the data that is readily observable, namely, 1970 through 1983. In order to examine the data, let us study the 1970 through 1984 portion of the chart. Please refer to Figure 4.2. A detailed examination of this chart now shows several specific cycles averaging 5–6 years in length when measured from low to low. A zigzag showing cycle trends and top-bottom measurements represents the cycle, and the figure appearing within the cycle is the approximate length in years and fractions measured from low to low. You can see that there is a fairly regular silver cycle running approximately 5–6 years on average during the 1970 through 1984 time frame.

Now let us follow the same procedure with the 1940 through 1970 price data to determine whether cyclic patterns were present at that time. Figure 4.3 shows silver prices' monthly cash average from 1940 to 1970. I have marked accordingly the 5–6 year cycle lows and highs so that you may readily observe them. As you can see, the cyclic patterns existed during the 1940 through 1970 period, although certain considerations (such as war) caused some disruption in the price cycle. Adding the various cycle lengths that have been isolated in Figures 4.2 and 4.3, we arrive at the figures shown in Figure 4.4.

$\bar{X}$ refers to the arithmetic mean of cycle lengths. Deviation refers to the number of years' (and/or fractions thereof) deviation from the average cycle length. The average deviation figure represents the average deviation that can be expected from the cycle, both plus and minus. You can see that the history of silver prices has been most impressive relative to cyclic length. It can be said that there is most certainly a 5–6 year period in silver prices and that it has been in existence since 1900, perhaps earlier. Lieutenant Commander David Williams has verified in his work the existence of many silver cycles well back to the 1700s and includes among his work the 5–6 year cycle.* Figure 4.5 is a reproduction of his silver cycles analysis showing technical features of silver chart formations as well as cycles of several different lengths in the silver market.

The same procedure can be followed for copper prices. Edward R. Dewey, who clearly demonstrated the existence of many cycles in the copper market, has, in fact, taken his study back to the 1700s to verify the existence of definitive and statistically verifiable cycles in copper. Here, also, the appearance of an approximate 5–6 year cycle has been demonstrated, along with the presence of several longer cycles, each reliable in its own right. Figure 4.6 illustrates the

* D. Williams, "Cycles in Silver, Gold and Economics," *Cycles,* May/June 1982, pp. 113–128.

Figure 4.1 Monthly cash average silver prices 1900–1984. (Reprinted with permission of MBH Commodity Advisors, Inc., P.O. Box 353, Winnetka, IL 60093.)

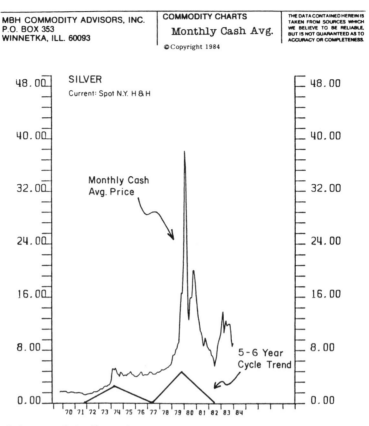

Figure 4.2   5–6 year cycle in silver prices.
(Reprinted with permission of MBH Commodity Advisors, Inc., P.O. Box 353, Winnetka, IL 60093.)

presence of several cycles in copper showing the approximate average length
between cycle lows.

Now let us follow the same "dissection" procedure we used with silver
prices to determine both the length and the existence of a 5–6 year rhythm in
copper prices. Figure 4.7 shows copper prices from 1970 through 1984. It also
illustrates the approximate 5–6 year cycle. Figure 4.8 shows the same analysis
from 1940 through 1969, and Figure 4.9 shows the same analysis from 1927
through 1952. You can see that the same procedure has now been followed for
copper prices, and that the copper market certainly conforms to the analysis
presented here. Figure 4.10 lists the copper cycle lengths, the average length,
and the deviation and average deviation of the arithmetic mean.

This demonstration shows quite clearly the cyclic price patterns in copper
since the 1900s and certainly supports the contention that copper prices are
subject to rhythmic fluctuation. Unfortunately, gold prices cannot be subjected
to the same analysis since their history is rather brief. The available statistics
on platinum prices are also rather limited and, therefore, my choice of silver
and copper is also one of necessity. It is reasonable to assume, however, that
silver, gold, platinum, palladium, and copper tend to follow the same basic

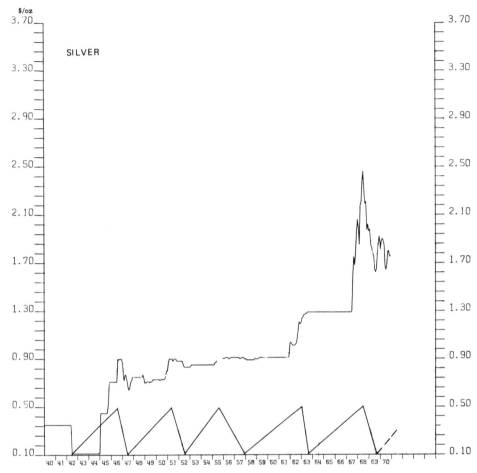

Figure 4.3 Year cycle in silver prices 1940–1970.
(Reprinted with permission of MBH Commodity Advisors, Inc., P.O. Box 353, Winnetka, IL 60093.)

Cycle Length (years)

5.6
6.2
5.4
5.7
5.1
SUM OF YEARS = 28.0
X = SUM OF YEARS DIVIDED BY NUMBER OF CYCLES = 5.6 year average cycle length.
The approximate silver cycle is, therefore, 5.6 years for the period studied.
DEVIATION = CYCLE − X

Figure 4.4 Cycle length averaging for 5–6 year silver cycle.

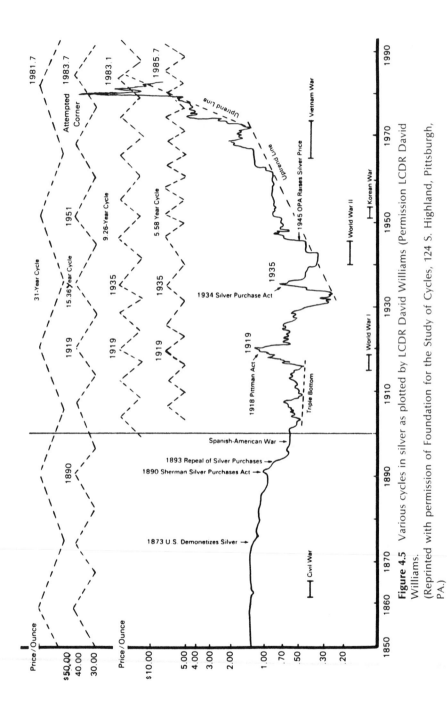

Figure 4.5 Various cycles in silver as plotted by LCDR David Williams (Permission LCDR David Williams.
(Reprinted with permission of Foundation for the Study of Cycles, 124 S. Highland, Pittsburgh, PA.)

54

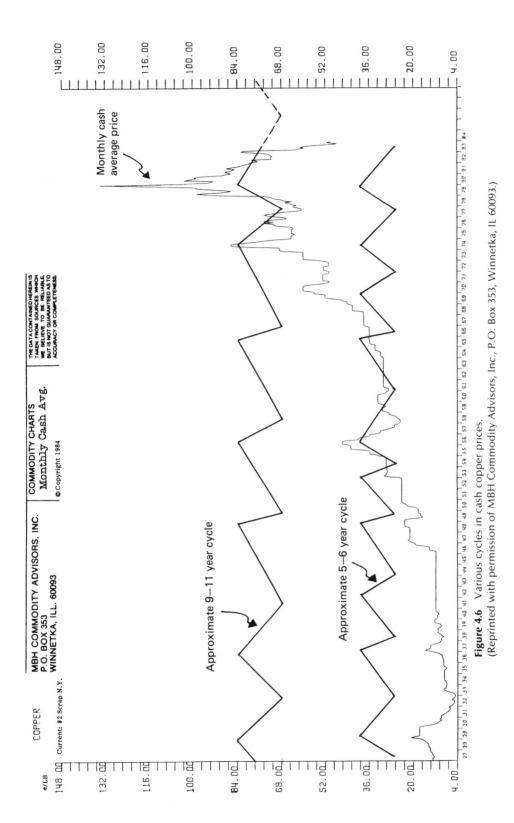

Figure 4.6 Various cycles in cash copper prices.
(Reprinted with permission of MBH Commodity Advisors, Inc., P.O. Box 353, Winnetka, IL 60093.)

55

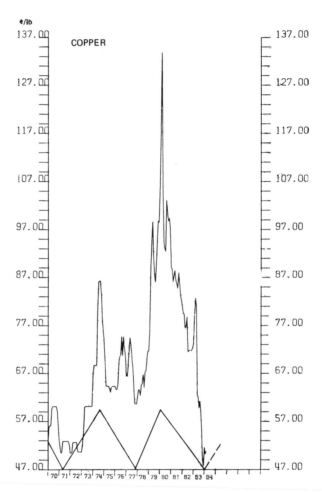

Figure 4.7 Copper cycles 1970–1984.
(Reprinted with permission of MBH Commodity Advisors, Inc., P.O. Box 353, Winnetka, IL 60093.)

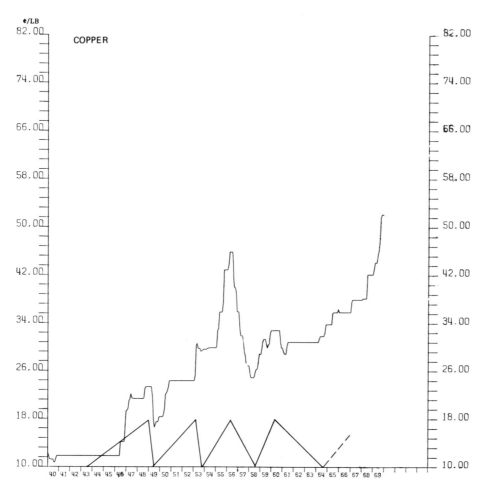

Figure 4.8 Copper cycles 1940–1969.
(Reprinted with permission of MBH Commodity Advisors, Inc., P.O. Box 353, Winnetka, IL 60093.)

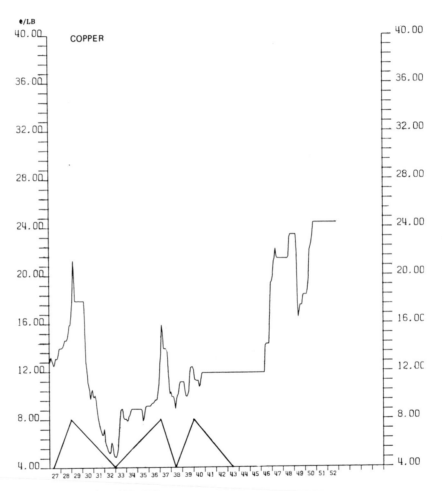

Figure 4.9 Copper cycles 1927–1952.
(Reprinted with permission of MBH Commodity Advisors, Inc., P.O. Box 353, Winnetka, IL 60093.)

Cycle Length (Years)

6.1
5.3
6.0
5.3
5.2
6.8
5.2
5.7
5.4
5.9

SUM OF YEARS = 56.9

X = SUM OF YEARS DIVIDED BY NUMBER OF CYCLES = 5.69 year average cycle length.

The approximate copper cycle is, therefore, 5.69 years for the period studied.

DEVIATION = CYCLE LENGTH − X

Figure 4.10 Computing the copper cycle average length.

cycle lengths. Figure 4.11 shows the price of copper and the price of silver on the same chart to compare recent price tendencies in history relative to the above point. You can see quite clearly that major price trends in both markets are similar. The same analysis performed on gold and platinum (Figure 4.12) and gold and copper (Figure 4.13) further emphasizes the closeness of cyclic behavior in metals. This is not to say that price magnitude in one market cannot exceed price magnitude in another (i.e., platinum gaining on gold in a bull market). My only purpose in making these comparisons is to demonstrate the relatively similar nature of price cycles in the metals as a group.

SHORT TERM, LONG TERM, INTERMEDIATE TERM— WHAT THEY MEAN

As you know, what we choose to define as "long term" or "short term" is a matter of opinion. We have just finished examining several cycles that I called long term. Some individuals may feel that these cycles are, in fact, relatively short term given such secular forces as the 50 to 60 year cycle in metals, the economy, and business. In fact, some researchers (see literature by the Foundation for the Study of Cycles*) claim the existence of cycles that are several hundred years in length. While I do not doubt the validity of work in cycles longer than the ones discussed in this text, I do believe that their degree of accuracy and relative length make them somewhat impractical for long-range investment purposes. Say, for example, that a 38 year cycle is discovered. Given an approximately 10% plus or minus degree of error in the timing of tops and bottoms, the cycle could be as much as 3.8 years earlier or 3.8 years later. This

---

* E. R. Dewey, *Cycles—Selected Writings* (Pittsburgh: Foundation for the Study of Cycles, 1970), pp. 578–579, 627, 749.

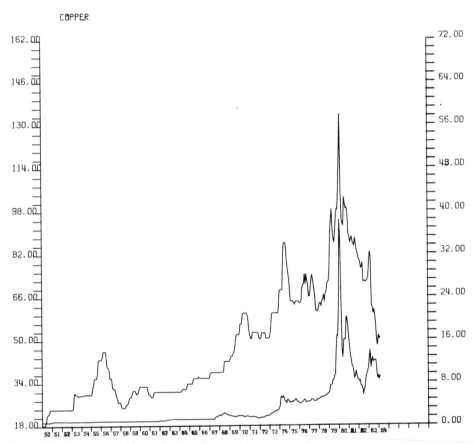

Figure 4.11 Copper and silver price trend comparison.
(Reprinted with permission of MBH Commodity Advisors, Inc., P.O. Box 353, Winnetka, IL 60093.)

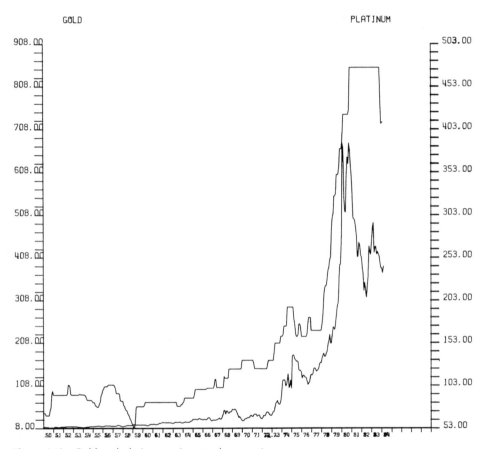

Figure 4.12 Gold and platinum price trend comparison.
(Reprinted with permission of MBH Commodity Advisors, Inc., P.O. Box 353, Winnetka, IL 60093.)

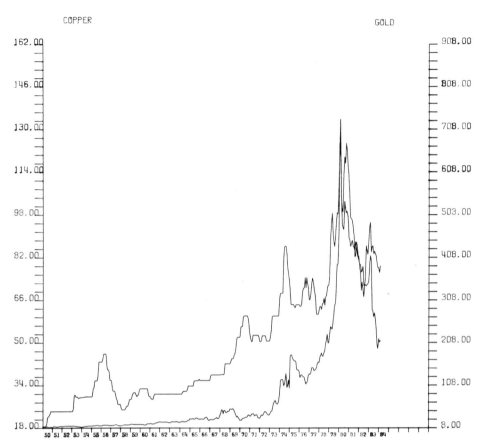

Figure 4.13 Gold and copper price trend comparison.
(Reprinted with permission of MBH Commodity Advisors, Inc., P.O. Box 353, Winnetka, IL 60093.)

covers a time span of 7.6 years. In other words, it is during a 7.6 year time frame that the cycle could reach its turning point. Such a lengthy time window is too panoramic, and it is not subject to the pragmatic considerations that must necessarily concern the investor. Even the cycles used in this book (i.e., 5–6 years and shorter) are somewhat on the long side, with ideal turning points being a plus or minus 10% of 6 years, or, therefore, yielding a 1.2 year time window. The 1.2 year time frame can be manageable, providing that there is a technique for focusing on a more restricted period of time through the use of other cyclic techniques.

One such technique is to examine cycles of shorter duration within the long-term cycle. Let us assume, for example, that the ideal cycle in silver is 5.5 years; 5.5 years is equal to 66 months. Sixty-six months is easily divisible into 6 cycles of 11 months each. It is also divisible into approximately 8 cycles of slighty more than 8 months each, or approximately 5 cycles of 13 months each. It would, therefore, be logical to search for cycles in silver running from 8–13 months in length when measured from low to low. Figure 4.14 shows a monthly price chart of silver back to the 1960s. Although there is variation from one low

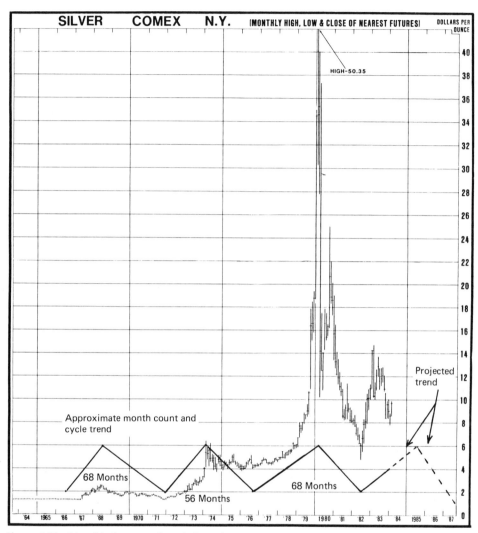

Figure 4.14 Monthly futures price of silver showing 5–6 year cycle lows and highs. (Reprinted with permission of Commodity Research Bureau, 75 Montgomery St., Jersey City, NJ 07302.)

to the next, you can see that the silver market has exhibited a reasonably good cycle that represents a fraction of the approximate 5.5 year cyclic pattern discussed earlier. (Fig. 4.16).

It is true, of course, that not all cycles fall perfectly within our ideal count; however, through the use of additional market-trend methods, it is possible to compensate for the degree of error inherent in determining cycle lengths. I realize that we are not dealing with an ideal situation, but let me hasten to add that in Chapter 8 we will deal with more realistic market situations that will allow you to obtain more direct experience with the technique. Let us take a similar example of intermediate-term cyclic pattern in the copper market. Figure 4.15 is a monthly price chart of copper dating back to the 1960s. I have marked the

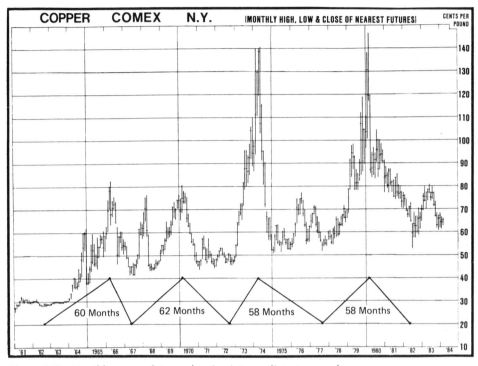

Figure 4.15 Monthly copper futures showing intermediate-term cycles.
(Reprinted with permission of Commodity Research Bureau, 75 Montgomery St., Jersey City, NJ 07302.)

approximate cyclic lows on the intermediate-term pattern to show how the cycle has functioned during this period of time. The last several years for copper and silver are examined from a closer persective in Figures 4.16 and 4.17. The gold market has a similar cyclic tendency, and I add once again a note of caution relative to the symmetry of cycles. I have repeatedly pointed out the importance of examining cycles from the perspective of irregularity as opposed to regularity. By this I mean, of course, that cycles tend to be irregular and not symmetrical. The human mind strives for symmetry, and many investors who follow cycles have difficulty visualizing a cyclic pattern that is not perfectly symmetrical. To implement and analyze cycles in the marketplace, however, it is necessary to abandon one's preconceived notions that the investment world or the economic world is comprised of symmetrical patterns. In fact, nature itself is not entirely symmetrical even though some patterns are perfectly equidistant from top to bottom and vice-versa. In the area of economics there are just too many inputs, too many variables, too much emotion, and too much political uncertainty to expect complete symmetry. Provided you can make the necessary mental adjustments and provided you can incorporate the appropriate compensatory tools, you will do well with the cycles as an aid to metal investments.

Within the 9–13 month cycle, there are also patterns of shorter duration. For example, the approximate 28-day cycle, 42-day cycle, 56-day cycle, and

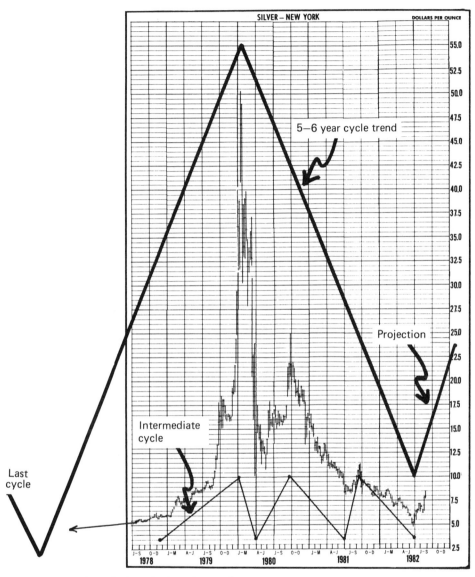

Figure 4.16 A closer look at the last silver cycle.
(Reprinted with permission of Commodity Research Bureau, 75 Montgomery St., Jersey City, NJ 07302.)

121-day cycle are well known patterns whose use has been popularized by short-term traders and speculators in the metals markets. (Since short-term trading is beyond the scope of this book, however, I will not spend time discussing these patterns.)

In summary, it has been demonstrated that cyclic patterns in the precious metals and copper markets are a viable and underlying force. It has also been

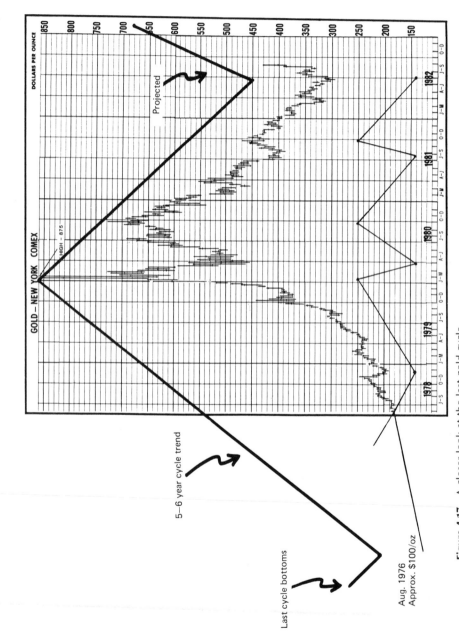

Figure 4.17 A closer look at the last gold cycle.
(Reprinted with permission of Commodity Research Bureau, 75 Montgomery St., Jersey City, NJ 07302.)

shown that cycles of shorter duration exist within the long-term cyclic patterns.

The long-term cyclic patterns are, in turn, part and parcel of even longer-term economic trends known as secular patterns. Since it is impossible to forecast cyclic tops and bottoms perfectly, and since it is impossible to have perfectly symmetrical cycles in the metals market (or, for that matter, in any other free market), it now becomes necessary to find a method by which the variation inherent in cyclic patterns can be filtered out in order to implement the cyclic pattern as part of a long-range investment program. This goal is best achieved through the use of timing indicators, which are discussed in the next chapter.

5

Timing in Conjunction with Cycles

Historically speaking, the point at which most investors make the wrong turn in the marketplace is the point at which they must actually enter or exit a market. It has been said that "timing is everything" and although this may not necessarily be as relevant to the long-term investor, it is certainly applicable to anyone with money to invest. Entering the market too soon can result in a number of difficulties, the greatest of which are financial and psychological. Entering a market too late, provided it is not terribly late, is not as potentially dangerous as entering a market too early. In fact, it is better to enter a market late than to enter too soon, since to enter too soon tends to constitute "bottom picking," which in and of itself can be a financially dangerous practice. The importance of market timing cannot be overstated or underrated. Many investors who are otherwise quite knowledgeable and appropriate in their investment decisions suffer from the inability to time purchases and sales as closely as necessary. For the futures trader, timing is quintessential. In futures trading, timing is "more than everything," since the very existence of a trader's account depends on virtually flawless timing. As we all know, this is an extremely difficult goal to achieve.

For the long-range investor, however, timing is not as critical since positions are entered with the intention of holding them for extended periods of time. Whereas a trader or speculator in the futures market may hold a position overnight or for as brief a period as several minutes, the investor may ride a position for several years. Consequently, the exact price at which initial market entry or exit is made becomes a less significant variable. In fact, based on the suggestions provided in this book, the long-term investor will frequently make a number of entries and exits during the appropriate time frame, thereby averaging his or her costs to a reasonable figure. The long-range investor approaches the marketplace with the understanding that at some point over the next several months or years a paper loss may be showing. The key to effective long-range investing, particularly in the areas of copper and the precious metals, is to average one's costs both on the way in and on the way out in order to achieve an overall price that is reasonably close to the actual market top or bottom. Perhaps the most unreasonable thing a long-range investor can do is to attempt entry and exit at the exact top or bottom of a market swing.

There are many different timing indicators. For the intermediate and short-term investor, timing is a crucial issue—preservation of capital is made possible by precise timing. For the long-range investor, however, timing is a less crucial issue. I do not mean to imply, however, that timing is unimportant to the long-term investor. Certainly we all want to buy at the lowest possible price and sell at the highest possible price. Since this is not often possible, the long-range investment approach I am proposing in this book seeks to average one's cost both when accumulating a position and when liquidating a position. To do this effectively I propose a combined approach that uses various timing principles as well as money management principles. The goal of such an approach is to accumulate positions within the lower 25% of the market bottom and to liquidate positions within 25% of the market top. I realize that this goal will not always be possible, but it is a goal toward which we must strive.

SOME TIMING INDICATORS

I mentioned earlier that many timing indicators can be used in selecting an entry point. I stress that these timing indicators are to be used only during the right time. By the "right time" I mean during the time period that is cyclically appropriate as a probable high or low based on the projection one has made. (The mechanics of the entire proposal will be discussed at a later point in this book. For now, however, let us focus on a few timing indicators.)

Monthly Up-side Price Reversal

Figure 5.1 shows the model for a monthly up-side price reversal. Up-side reversals tend to happen at cyclic lows and down-side reversals tend to happen at cyclic highs. Such reversals and their variations in connection with cycles for short-term trading have already been discussed in my text, *The Handbook of Commodity Cycles—A Window on Time*. Figure 5.2 shows the monthly down-side price reversal in general form. Figures 5.3 and 5.4 give real time examples of monthly up-side and down-side reversals at major cyclic lows and highs. I think you will agree that a connection appears to exist between the cycles and the two reversal states. It certainly seems that down-side reversals are most likely to be valid at cycle tops and up-side reversals are most apt to be valid at cycle lows. *Note that I am using monthly reversals.* The formula for determining a reversal is quite simple. To form a monthly up-side reversal, prices must

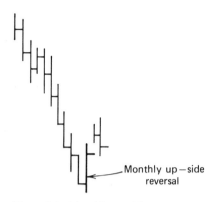

Figure 5.1 Monthly up-side price reversal.

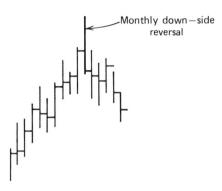

Figure 5.2 Monthly down-side price reversal.

Figure 5.3 Some monthly down-side reversals at major highs.
(Reprinted with permission of Commodity Research Bureau, 75 Montgomery St., Jersey City, NJ 07302.)

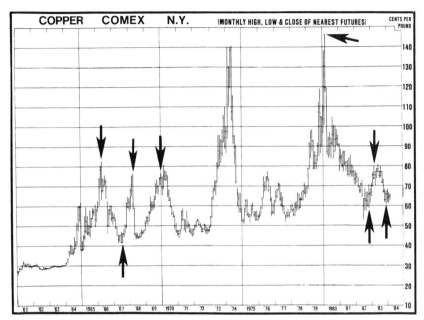

Figure 5.4 Monthly up-side and down-side reversals at major highs and lows.
(Reprinted with permission of Commodity Research Bureau, 75 Montgomery St., Jersey City, NJ 07302.)

trade lower than they did in the previous month; however, their closing price for the month (last price of the month) must be higher than the last closing price of the previous month. The reverse holds true for down-side monthly reversals.

Not the Only Indicators

Though not all tops and bottoms are identified by such reversals, a significant relationship exists between the proximity of monthly reversals and cyclic lows and highs. Hence, one thing a long-term investor must look for during the time window of a low or high is a monthly up-side or down-side reversal. The monthly reversal is one of the items on my checklist of things to watch for during the proper time frame. The proper time frame is, of course, the period of time during which a major low or high is expected. The reversals do not always come at the precise high or low. At times they come slightly prior to or slightly after the top or bottom. At times, in fact, they do not come at all. This is why I use additional indicators on my checklist of confirming signals.

The Low to High or High to Low Signal

Another signal I suggest you add to your checklist of things to look at is the *low to high* close signal when a cycle low is expected, and the *high to low* close

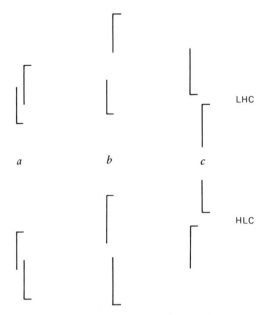

Figure 5.5   Low/high close signal model (LHC) and high/low close signal model (HLC).

signal when a top is expected. These signals are shown in diagram form (Figure 5.5), and are explained more fully in relationship to the cycles in *The Handbook of Commodity Cycles—A Window on Time*. Suffice it to say that these signals tend to appear at major tops and/or bottoms. It is not necessary for prices to close exactly on the low one month and exactly on their high the next month (or vice-versa). I use an approximate 10% leeway. In other words, if the closing price is within 10% of the monthly low or within 10% of the monthly high, this is sufficient to form a signal. The theory is, of course, that by closing at one extreme in one month and on the other extreme in the next month, the market has probably been purged of weak investors and the public while professionals then enter. Though this is not a 100% indicator, it appears to have validity at cyclic tops and bottoms both over the short term as well as over the long term.

Each of the two-month combinations shown in Figure 5.5 (i.e., *a, b,* and *c*) constitute a signal. Note that I have shown exact closes on the high or low, but do not forget the 10% leeway I give the indicator. In actual practice these signals look as shown in Figure 5.6. This chart shows arrows pointing to *high/low* close at tops and arrows pointing to *low/high* close at bottoms.

Combined Signals

It is, of course, possible that signals will combine to give low/high close and monthly up-side reversal at the same time or vice-versa. I attribute more validity to such combinations and have marked several of them on Figure 5.7. Again,

Figure 5.6 Low/high and high/low close signals at tops and bottoms.
(Reprinted with permission of Commodity Research Bureau, 75 Montgomery St., Jersey City, NJ
07302.)

it should be noted that *not all bottoms or tops are formed on such signals;
however, such signals attain their validity by proximity to major cycle turns.*

Penetration of Resistance/Support

Whereas tops tend to be made on spikes, many bottoms are likely to be extended, base building, or rounding in character. Another method of confirming
turns, primarily those from cycle lows or bottoms, is to use a resistance line
drawn above the highest highs during a period of price consolidation. Those familiar with traditional charting methods will know precisely what I mean. For
those who need a little instruction, Figure 5.8 provides the necessary "real
time" examples, taking a close-up look at several bottoms in the market. The

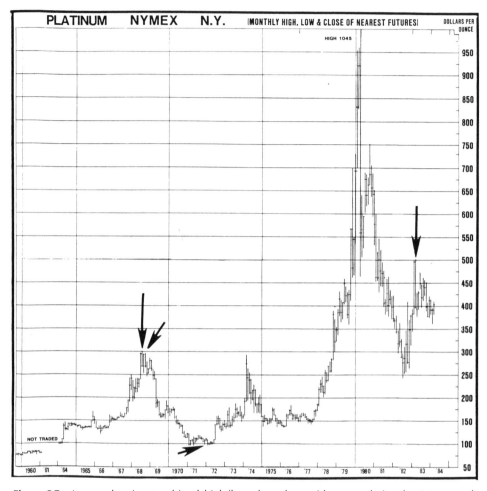

Figure 5.7 Arrows showing combined high/low close down-side reversal signals at tops, and low/high close up-side reversal signals bottoms.
(Reprinted with permission of Commodity Research Bureau, 75 Montgomery St., Jersey City, NJ 07302.)

rule is quite simple. After prices enter an ideal low time frame and form a "congestion" or support area of at least four months' duration, a resistance line is drawn above the highest of the intramonth highs. After the price for any given month thereafter closes above the resistance line, this indicates a probable turn to the up side. I stress that this signal is one of several *confirming* signals. It is something to add to the proposed checklist of market patterns that will be evaluated during the time frame of a major turn in prices.

Timing signals, are, therefore, important in *confirming* a low or high. In the marketplace history does not repeat itself in the same way each and every time. If this were the case I would not be writing this book since there would be nothing to teach and nothing to learn. All things would be clear and there would, more likely than not, be no market since prices would not be subject to human psychology and emotion. At any rate, the indicators discussed in this

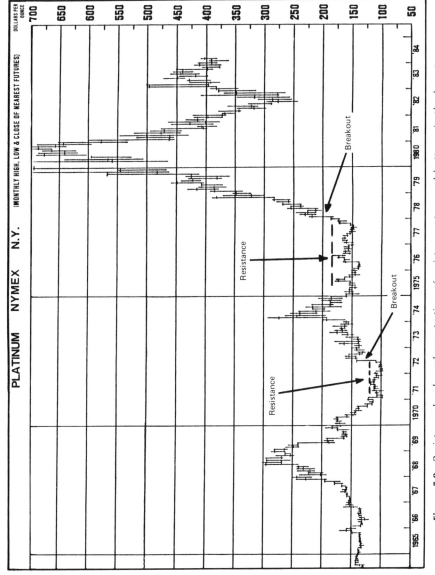

Figure 5.8 Resistance levels and penetration of resistance at several bottoms in the long-term platinum cycle.
(Reprinted with permission of Commodity Research Bureau, 75 Montgomery St., Jersey City, NJ 07302.)

chapter are only three of several that will go into the proposed list I have provided for long-term investors. Chapter 6 discusses moving average indicators. The essence of timing indicators is either to confirm or deny the bottom of a cycle. Indicators work in conjunction with the cycles and will help overcome the natural tendency of cycles to be a little early or a little late. (Chapter 8 will review this information in checklist form.)

6

Moving Averages and Cycles

Many traders and investors are familiar with moving averages. Although they do not necessarily understand all the mathematics involved, they certainly know that moving average systems can help the trader enter and exit a given market at appropriate turning points. The essence of moving average systems is that the moving averages change direction after the market has made a turn. Quite naturally, this means that a certain amount of price movement and profit will be sacrificed in favor of safety. In general, moving average systems will perform the best in markets showing long-term trends, whereas they will perform the worst in markets showing choppy or "whipsaw" type of behavior. Moving average systems are many and varied; some systems use combinations of moving averages, while others use variations of moving averages known as *oscillators*. The purpose of having a timing indicator in conjunction with the cycles is to permit optimum market entry and exit, sacrificing the minimal amount of potential profit while increasing safety to the maximum.

There are, of course, many techniques by which this can be achieved: timing indicators, trading indicators, overbought/oversold indicators, crossover systems, relative value indicators, and point and figure charts can all be used as methods by which timing can be optimized in the marketplace. (Some of these were discussed in Chapter 5.) Certainly, as the computer becomes more accessible to the average trader, such techniques will develop, prosper, and multiply. It is perhaps a truism in the market, as well as in other areas of life, that the old standby techniques are frequently the best. Certainly, if they are still in use today, then they have most likely survived the greatest test of all—the test of time. Moving averages have existed for quite some time, and many of the more successful stock and commodity systems use moving average timing for their base.

It is certainly not within my ability to guarantee anyone complete success with moving average systems in combination with cycles, nor is it my intention to suggest that this is the best combination. I have, however, witnessed a sufficient number of systems in operation, to the extent that my experience tells me what can and will work, as well as what is not likely to succeed.

Before examining the basics of moving averages in relation to long-term price movement, however, I would like to discuss how moving averages are constructed. Richard Donchian, often referred to as the "Father of Moving Averages," familiarized the trading community many years ago with moving averages. In a now classic article, Mr. Donchian discussed the early versions of his moving average indicators.* For explanatory purposes, he also produced the accompanying chart (Fig. 6.1) to illustrate the major aspects of his moving average technique. In addition, Mr. Donchian delineated the following basic rules, which must be used in connection with moving averages.

Since the late 1950s, there have been many additions to, and modifications of, basic moving average techniques. The system however, is still ultimately simple, in terms of both calculating the specific moving average numbers and in the objectivity of its application. Perhaps the greatest asset of the moving average system is its objectivity. This would, of course, hold true for any technical trading system since it is the ultimate goal of technical trading to remove subjectivity and replace it with objective decisions regarding trade selection. (Anyone interested in the precise manner of calculating and applying moving average rules should consult some of the more recent texts on moving averages, specifically Kaufman.†)

In effect, the moving average is calculated by adding together a given number of prices and dividing by the number of prices used. The first moving average, therefore, in a series is calculated by adding the number of prices defined by the moving average length. Specifically, a 10 week moving average is calculated by adding 10 weekly prices and dividing by the number 10. The next moving average in the series is calculated by subtracting the first number in the original series of observations from the subtotal (prior to division), then adding the 11th price observation to the subtotal, and dividing by 10. What we have done, then, is to drop the oldest bit of data and add the newest bit of data. In short, the average has "moved": it has, in effect, shifted forward in time to account for the last 10 prices. The average moves forward in time and lags behind price. It is precisely this time lag that makes the moving average useful. The moving average is, in effect, a desensitized version of price. It smooths the price out by removing most erratic ups and down, and it tends to change direction slower than does price.

The theory is that once price falls below its moving average (of whatever length one has decided), this is technically an indication that price cannot sustain its up trend, and that a down trend must necessarily follow. There is no indication about how long the down trend might last, but in purely technical terms one could say that the down trend could last until price crosses back above moving average, indicating that trend has now turned higher. You can well appreciate the fact that the shorter the moving average length, the more

* Richard D. Donchian, "Trend-Following Methods in Commodity Price Analysis," *Commodity Year Book* (1957), pp. 35–47.
† J. Kaufman. *Commodity Trading Systems and Methods* (New York: Wiley-Interscience, 1978).

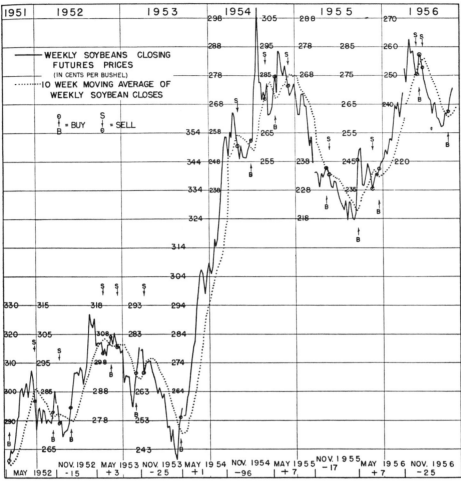

Figure 6.1   Donchian's chart of 10-week moving average of soybean futures with buy/sell signals (CRB, 1957, pg. 37).
(Reprinted with permission of Commodity Research Bureau, 75 Montgomery St., Jersey City, NJ 07302.)

crossovers there will be, and the longer the moving average, the less crossovers there will be. Longer-term and shorter-term moving averages each have their benefits and their drawbacks. Hence, the true art of applying moving averages resides in selecting the moving average length that is optimum for the given market being studied.

Figure 6.2 shows a monthly moving average plotted against monthly cash average. As you will notice, the moving average is a smooth line, and the price is the more jagged line. I have also marked some moving average crossovers to illustrate ideal market turns as assessed by the crossover signals. In other words, price cross under moving average is an indication to sell, whereas price cross over moving average is an indication to buy. Note that I have said nothing yet about risk, degree of stop, price objective, time objective, or strength of the move. Figures 6.3*a, b,* and *c* show the same market plotted with different

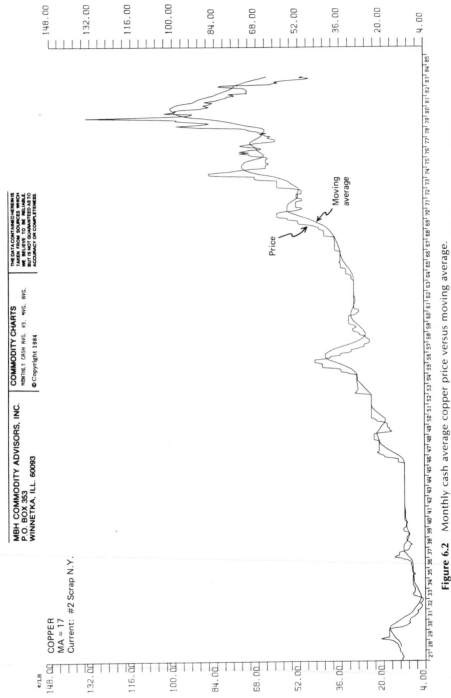

Figure 6.2 Monthly cash average copper price versus moving average. (Reprinted with permission of MBH Commodity Advisors, Inc., P.O. Box 353, Winnetka, IL 60093.)

80

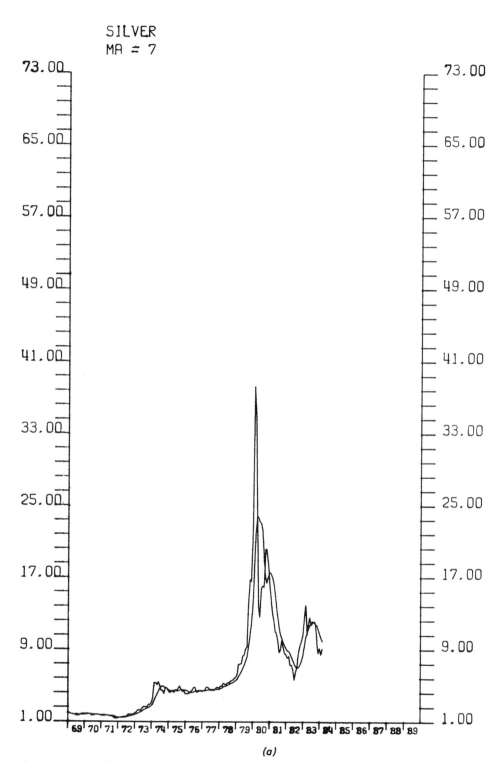

Figure 6.3a Monthly cash average silver price 1969–1984 plotted against three different moving averages.

(Reprinted with permission of MBH Commodity Advisors, Inc., P.O. Box 353, Winnetka, IL 60093.)

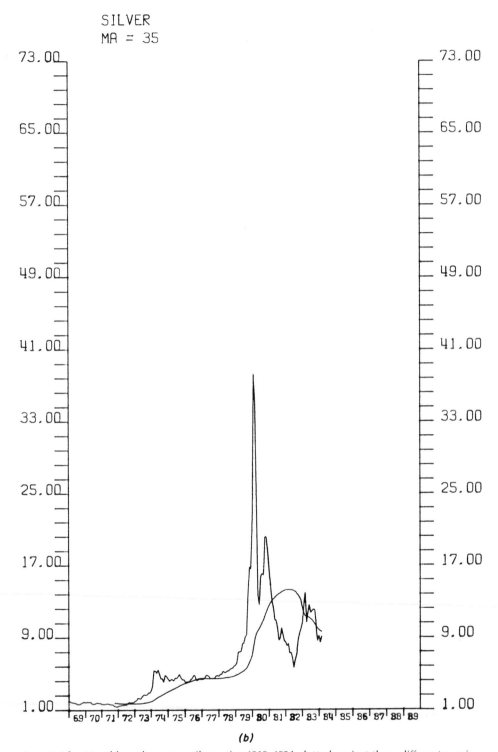

Figure 6.3 b Monthly cash average silver price 1969–1984 plotted against three different moving averages.

(Reprinted with permission of MBH Commodity Advisors, Inc., P.O. Box 353, Winnetka, IL 60093.)

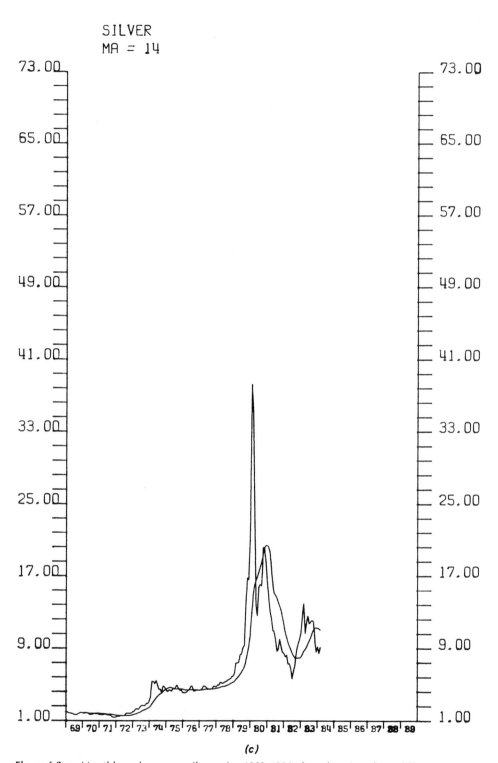

Figure 6.3 c Monthly cash average silver price 1969–1984 plotted against three different moving averages.
(Reprinted with permission of MBH Commodity Advisors, Inc., P.O. Box 353, Winnetka, IL 60093.)

moving averages of different lengths to illustrate my point that selection of moving average length is a critical variable in successful use of the moving average system. You can see that the moving average selected in Figure 6.3a is much too short, resulting in many crossovers, and, in effect, an indicator that has no practical use. Figure 6.3b shows a moving average that is too long. In essence, there are virtually no signals here because there are few crossovers. Figure 6.3c shows a more ideal moving average, giving a reasonable number of entry and exit signals. Various techniques can be used to determine the appropriate length of moving average one would want to employ in analyzing a given market. As a rule of thumb, the best overall method I have found is trial and error. One must study the history of a given market and see which moving average has performed most consistently at major tops and bottoms. Certainly, the criteria for selecting a good moving average should take two things into consideration. First, the moving average must turn reasonably close to a major top or bottom in the market; and, second, the moving average must result in the minimum number of "false" signals during the subsequent up or down trend.

Figure 6.3a shows a moving average plotted against price. Although this moving average did a wonderful job in picking tops and bottoms, it did a poor job in remaining consistently above or below price subsequent to the major top or bottom. This was technically as valuable as having no signal at all, because, at the time each contrary crossover occurred, the trader or investor would not have been certain whether a new trend was beginning. (Ways to avoid this problem are described in subsequent chapters.) Figure 6.3b shows the same market for the same period of time using a different moving average, one that results in significantly fewer "false" signals.

Another general rule for selecting moving averages in conjunction with cycles is to select the moving average that is approximately one-half or one-quarter of the cycle length. Consequently, a cycle length of six years would probably be used best in conjunction with a moving average of approximately three years' length. Because three years' length translates into 36 months, a 36 month moving average could be used. Experience teaches, however, that a 36 month moving average is somewhat too high and a 25% cycle length moving average might prove more appropriate. Hence, the next length one would attempt should be 25% of 6 years, or, therefore, one-quarter times 72 months equals 13 months moving average. Assume now that the gold cycle runs approximately 5½–6 years low to low. Figure 6.4 shows the gold index/gold chart plotted against a 36 month moving average, and Figure 6.5 shows the same chart (gold index/gold chart) plotted against a 13 month moving average. As you can readily see, the 13 month moving average is considerably more responsive and substantially more pragmatic than the 36 month moving average in Figure 6.4. For the sake of comparison, Figure 6.6 shows the same gold index/gold chart, plotted with a 7 month moving average. The 7 month moving average, as you can see, is too short for practical application.

In addition to the simple moving averages discussed above, there are variations on the moving average theme, some of which, although not necessarily by design, may confuse the average investor. Two moving averages, for example, can be used in combination to provide other types of signals, some of

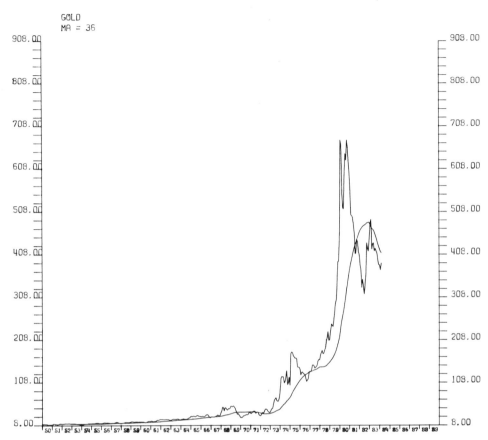

Figure 6.4 Gold index/gold monthly average plotted against 36 month average. (Reprinted with permission of MBH Commodity Advisors, Inc., P.O. Box 353, Winnetka, IL 60093.)

which are based on the requirement that both moving averages head in the same direction to confirm a crossover. Other systems use crossovers of one moving average, and the other as their timing indicator. Perhaps an individual who is considerably more adept with moving averages than I am can refine my cyclic moving average combination, thereby improving timing considerably. (If so, I would certainly like to hear from you since I will never be too experienced to learn something new or too successful to improve.)

Figure 6.7 shows silver prices (monthly cash average) plotted against two moving averages. By using two moving averages of different lengths as a check and balance system, one can filter out false signals by selling short or liquidating a position only when both moving averages are above price or by buying or covering shorts only when both moving averages are below price. The double moving average technique, although more time consuming in application, is beneficial to the individual who prefers more confirmation of a turn in market trends.

Moving averages can be used with short-term and long-term cycles, and they can also be applied to intermediate-term price cycles. Shown in tabular

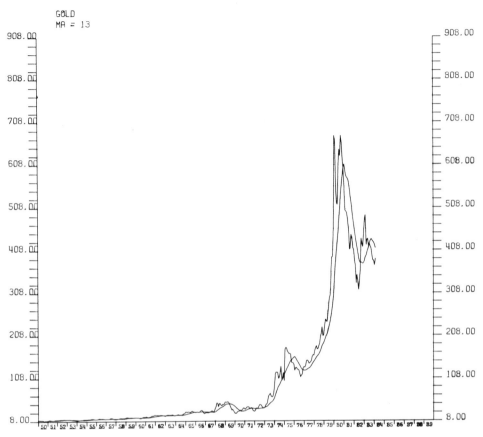

Figure 6.5 Gold index/gold monthly average plotted against 13 month moving average. (Reprinted with permission of MBH Commodity Advisors, Inc., P.O. Box 353, Winnetka, IL 60093.)

form (Fig. 6.8) are the moving averages that I have found optimum in the various precious metals and copper. I have also indicated the double moving averages that are likely to be more successful.

Now that we have examined moving averages and double moving averages, let us spend just a few moments discussing moving average oscillators as indicators of overbought/oversold markets' conditions. The oscillator is not a timing indicator; rather, it is a confirmatory indicator that is likely to serve you well in confirming that a market is low enough to begin a turn up or high enough to begin a turn down. As you will recall, I mentioned previously that major turns in most markets are concomitant with severely overbought or oversold conditions. Precisely what do I mean by "overbought" and "oversold"? There is, to my knowledge, no objective single statement that can suffice as a definition of the above conditions. What is it that makes a market oversold? What is it that makes a market overbought? Are these terms arbitrarily employed by those who have a vested interest in market tops and bottoms? Or can specific indicators mechanically define overbought/oversold market conditions? I am quite certain that if you ask 10 technicians their definition of these

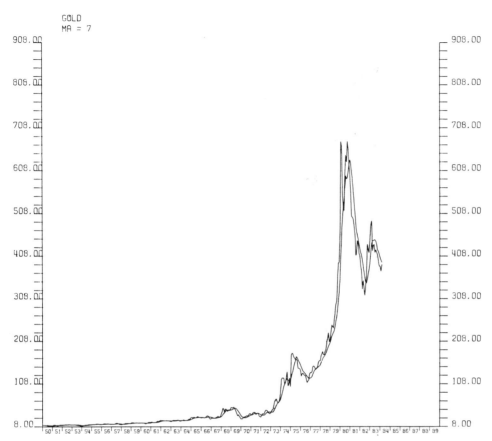

Figure 6.6 Gold index/gold monthly average plotted against a 7 month moving average. (Reprinted with permission of MBH Commodity Advisors, Inc., P.O. Box 353, Winnetka, IL 60093.)

terms you will probably receive 10 different answers. Each will contain, however, one common thread. That thread is the concept that an oversold condition arises from essentially psychological liquidation of positions and emotional short selling in fear that the bottom will "never come." An oversold condition is, therefore, in general terms, a condition whereby prices have fallen to such a significant extent that they are no longer realistic in terms of the underlying supply-demand characteristics of the given commodity. It is not unusual, for example, to see futures prices fall well below cash market prices at major market bottoms. In other words, speculators and those liquidating long positions obtain such an intensity of negative consensus that their combined selling drives prices disproportionately below their intrinsic value.

Perhaps one objective way to measure this phenomenon on a fundamental level is to assess all the appropriate fundamental inputs, such as demand, supply, storage, anticipated use, imports, exports, economic conditions, interest rates, and a plethora of other factors. Since most of these facts are either unavailable to the average individual or too time consuming for the average individual to gather, we must find another way to determine what is realistic in

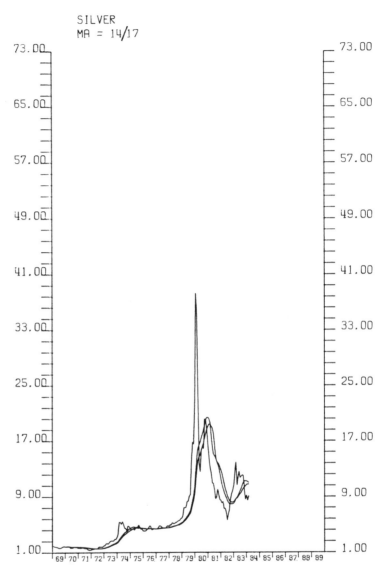

Figure 6.7 Silver monthly cash average 1969–1984 plotted against two moving averages. (Reprinted with permission of MBH Commodity Advisors, Inc., P.O. Box 353, Winnetka, IL 60093.)

terms of prices. The other side of the coin is, of course, an overbought condition. Overbought conditions have, during the last three decades, been more common than oversold conditions because three world economies have been in a generally inflationary trend from 1948 through 1980. Simply stated, an overbought condition is the exact opposite of an oversold condition. Overbought conditions, however, tend to be significantly less obvious when they occur because there is theoretically no limit to how high prices can go, whereas there is a theoretical limit to how low prices can go (and that is zero). As market tops, optimism reigns supreme and what seems to be a never-ending supply of funds

MARKET	MOVING AVERAGE 1	MOVING AVERAGE 2	COMMENTARY
COPPER	17 MONTHS	21 MONTHS	good historical reliability
SILVER	13 MONTHS	18 MONTHS	average historical reliability
GOLD	13 MONTHS	18 MONTHS	data history is limited
PLATINUM	13 MONTHS	18 MONTHS	good reliability

Figure 6.8 Table of ideal moving average lengths by market.

supports the market on each decline. Traders often grow weary waiting for tops to develop and many, at the last moment, decide to throw in the towel and join the long side.

One way to determine how bullish the pubic is has been developed and refined by R. Earl Hadaday. In his book, entitled *Contrary Opinion,* Mr. Hadaday discusses in specific detail the methods that he has been using since the 1960s to assess the level of bullish and bearish consensus of opinion.* Originally, his work in the futures market was a variation on the original theories of contrary opinion that have previously gained wide interest in the stock market.

My reason for mentioning bullish consensus and contrary opinion in connection with overbought/oversold indicators is that frequently the level of bullish sentiment will indicate when a market has become overbought and/or oversold. Typically, a strong agreement between market newsletters and traders still signals sufficient conditions for an extreme in price. Traditionally, when 75% or more of those traders surveyed agree that prices are indeed going lower, the probability is quite high that, in fact, they are bottoming and most likely oversold. Such turning points generally arrive in conjunction with cyclic lows and shortly thereafter it is often the case that prices turn higher and penetrate their moving averages. Bullish opinion of a high level (typically in excess of 80%) usually triggers a top in the market. Few markets can sustain bullish consensus readings of 80% or more for more than several weeks' time. Recently some traders have started using 16 week moving averages of bullish and bearish consensus figures as a method by which cyclic turning points can be isolated. Shown in Figure 6.9 is a chart from Mr. Hadaday's book illustrating the relationship between bullish consensus and market turns. It is quite obvious that contrary opinion (i.e., bullish consensus readings) can be a useful tool at important tops and bottoms in the marketplace.

Another indicator of overbought/oversold is, as mentioned above, the moving average oscillator. Quite simply, the moving average oscillator consists of two moving averages subtracted from one another and plotted against price. In effect, the oscillator tends to detrend prices, accentuating the peaks and valleys that generally cluster in a similar support or resistance zone. Typically, an oscillator that reads under zero marks an oversold condition, whereas an oscillator reading in excess of 100 marks an overbought condition. As I metioned earlier, however, it is more difficult to determine market tops using an oscillator than it is to determine market bottoms using an oscillator.

A brief illustration will explain precisely what I mean by the above state-

* Earl Hadaday, *Contrary Opinion* (Pasadena, CA: Hadaday Publications, 1983).

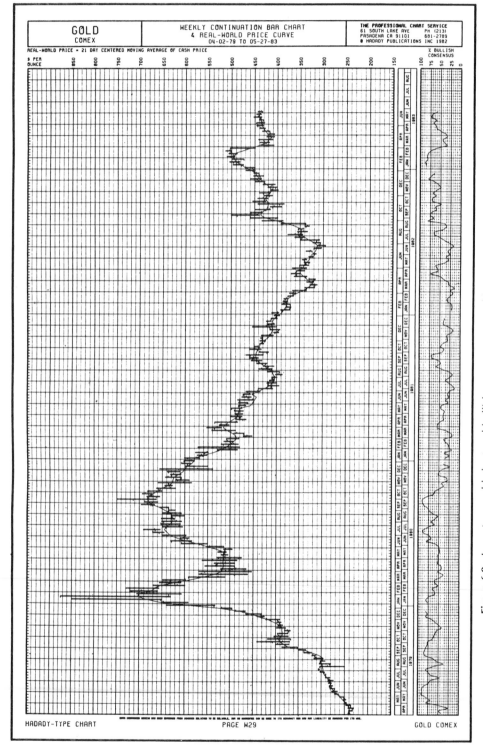

Figure 6.9 Long-term gold chart and bullish consensus as used by R. E. Hadaday. (Reprinted with permission of Hadady Publications, Inc., 61 South Lake Avenue, Pasadena, CA 91101.)

ment. Figure 6.10 shows *Standard and Poor's* composite average on a monthly basis dated back to the 1940s plotted against a price oscillator comprised of two moving averages shown at the top left of the chart. The shaded areas at the bottom of the chart (marked oversold) show how the oscillator acted at major market lows over the last 40 plus years. Arrows pointing up from each oversold bottom condition point to lows of significance during this time frame. Also shown in Figure 6.10 is the trend line of connecting tops illustrating overbought condition. You can readily observe that overbought market conditions are not as easily identified as oversold conditions. The reason for this situation's existence is simply understood if one takes into consideration the fact that the secular trend of prices in *Standard and Poor's* (i.e., stocks) has been up for most of the time period studied. In more normal market conditions where prices show more two-sided trends, oscillators are more useful in identifying tops based on overbought conditions.

Figure 6.11 shows copper prices in their period of relative stability during which there were ups and downs (albeit less violent ones than has been the case from 1970 through 1984). Regardless of the market studied, moving average oscillators can serve as useful additions to the logical sequence of decisions that must be made at cyclic turning points. Chapter 7 illustrates the combined use of technical tools discussed in this chapter and their relationship to the overall proposed strategy in metals.

The selection of moving averages that best illustrates overbought/oversold conditions is another more or less artistic process based on experience and feel

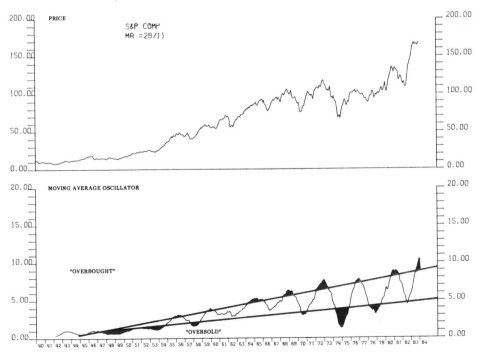

Figure 6.10 *S&P* index monthly average (top) versus moving average oscillator of price (bottom). (Reprinted with permission of MBH Commodity Advisors, Inc., P.O. Box 353, Winnetka, IL 60093.)

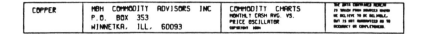

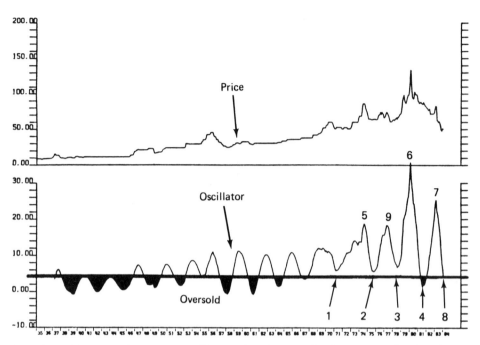

Figure 6.11   Copper moving average oscillator and explanatory details. In terms of analysis here is what I see. An oscillator reading of zero, minus, or close to zero often indicates oversold conditions with probability of a rally being relatively high. The 1935–1964 time frame for copper showed many instances of oversold prices, but the overall trend during this time was fairly stable and price moves were relatively small. But bottoms 1–4 were all "oversold" lows, and rallies followed. We are now at bottom marked #8. My conclusion is that the market is long-term oversold with a rally of substance now due. As far as tops go numbers 5–7 and 9 were all "overbought" tops.

for the market. A rule of thumb that serves well is to select two moving averages that are quite different in magnitude: for example, a long moving average versus a short-term moving average comprises perhaps the best combination, whereas two moving averages close in time may not necessarily illustrate the overbought/oversold conditions as clearly as will two distinctly different averages. Figure 6.12 shows my selection of moving average lengths for the oscillators in each of the markets listed. You are by no means obligated to adhere to these lengths; however, I have done sufficient testing to convince myself that the selected lengths are desirable in computing the oscillators.

To review what has been discussed in this chapter, remember the following:

1. Moving averages are technical timing indicators that turn after markets change trends.

MARKET	OSCILLATOR LENGTHS
SILVER	13 and 29
GOLD	13 and 27
PLATINUM	15 and 24
COPPER	12 and 26

Figure 6.12   Oscillator moving averages for metals.

2. Moving averages can be used to verify cycle turns.

3. The selection of moving averages is more or less a trial and error method.

4. Moving averages function on price versus moving average crossovers.

5. Two moving averages can often work better than one moving average alone.

6. Bullish/bearish consensus can be used to determine overbought/oversold conditions.

7. Oscillators can also be used to spot important cyclic turning points primarily on the bottom side as opposed to the top side.

7

Combining Cycles with Moving Averages

In the previous chapter, I examined in considerable detail the manner in which moving averages are constructed and their various applications in determining when to buy and when to sell. Although opinions differ regarding the most efficacious use of moving averages, I believe that the suggestions made in this chapter, along with the historical performance of these suggestions, will convince you that there is yet another way in which the various moving average indictors and combinations can be useful to the long-term trader.

In effect, the use of cycles in and of themselves frequently fails to provide as much information on precise timing as the investor needs. The degree of error (cycle topping or bottoming early or late) with cycles is such that additional indicators are necessary to employ them completely in a long-range investment approach. Chapter 5 studied the relationships between classic timing signals and market tops/bottoms. These concepts are discussed more fully in my publication, *The Handbook of Commodity Cycles—A Window on Time.* Now, however, I have completed additional research that was in process during the last several years. These new findings focus on moving average combinations with cycles as an additional timing method for the long-range trader.

Consider for a moment the following "model" of the cyclic approach:

Cycle Projection + Timing Indicators = Buy/Sell/Hold Decision

Basically, if we know the approximate cycle and if we project the cycle and apply timing indicators, we can make an educated decision about buying or selling. The timing decision is assisted by a proposed checklist of technical indicators (as previously explained) that assist in the decision-making process.

As you can see, the decision-making process is clearly motivated and stimulated by timing. Timing, as always, is the most crucial factor confronting traders and investors. But the timing issue is not nearly as important to the long-range investor as it is to the short-term trader. If, for example, an individual is working with a cycle that repeats itself only every 14 days, then a 3 day error in timing either way constitutes almost one-half the cycle length. The investor who is waiting for a 5–6 year low in gold prices and happens to buy one month early will not necessarily be under the same pressure as the short-term trader who made an almost 50% error in timing judgment. In addition, the long-term trader will make different use of margin than will the short-term speculator, which will, in effect, allow him or her to ride his or her position for a considerably longer period of time before it becomes necessary to sell out, if a loss actually must be taken. By adding additional elements of timing to the cycle, the long-term investor can narrow his or her market entry and exit to a finer point, thereby increasing potential profit and riding losing positions accumulated at the bottoms of cycles for shorter periods of time before a definite market turn occurs.

The purpose, then, of using a timing indicator in conjunction with the cycle is to improve on the accuracy of the cycle itself. The combination of moving average, moving average crossover, and cycles, described in this book, comprises the essence of my *cyclic investing technique*. The basic sequence of steps that will be proposed in this chapter and amplified in the next chaper consists of the following:

1. Determine cycle lengths.
2. Determine last cycle low and high.
3. Project time window.

STEP 1: DETERMINE CYCLE LENGTHS

Figure 7.1 shows the cycle lengths that I have been using in my studies of precious metals and copper. You will note that the time frame 5–6 years is quite reasonable for gold, silver, and platinum. Palladium has a limited data history and, consequently, no long-term cycle is listed here. The best suggestion I can make is to use the same lengths shown by other precious metals, namely 5–6 years. Copper shows an approximate 5.9 year cycle and a fairly good 2.7 year cycle. All the metals have 9 to 13 month cycles. In addition, there are short-term cycles running considerably less than 9 months; however, these are beyond the scope of the present study and do not fit into the type of analysis we are seeking to perform. After you have selected the proper cycle length, determine which of the markets and the length of the cycles you wish to follow. Within the guidelines of my model portfolio (Chapter 10) it is possible to have positions in all the metals at the same time.

It is also important to have current charts that are updated regularly so that you will know precisely where you stand in the cycle. In this respect, I suggest the following:

MARKET	LONG TERM CYCLE	INTERMEDIATE TERM CYCLE #1	#2
COPPER	5.9 yrs	14–17 months	9–13 months
SILVER	5.5 yrs	14–17 months	9–13 months
GOLD	6.3 yrs	14–17 months	9–13 months
PLATINUM	5.5 yrs	14–17 months	9–13 months
PALLADIUM	5.5 yrs*	14–17 months	NA

*data history on palladium is not sufficient to permit a good analysis

Figure 7.1 Cycle lengths in metals.

1. Monthly cash average charts, such as those used in this book, should be acquired. (They can be purchased for a nominal price from my office or you may keep them up to date starting from scratch, on your own, if you have access to the necessary data.)
2. Intermediate-term cycle lows and highs should be kept by having a weekly closing price chart of the nearest futures contract. As an alternative, you may use weekly, high, low, close of the nearest futures contract to plot and spot the intermediate-term cycles. Such charts are available through most popular commodity charting services.
3. You should also have a separate set of charts on which you keep a moving average indicator both for the intermediate term and the long term.
4. You should also have an oscillator chart of the appropriate moving average combination for each market plotted against price. Samples of these charts have been shown in Figures 6.10, 6.11, and 6.12.

Once your chart work is current and being regularly maintained, have your charts show the last cycle low and cycle high for each of the markets on the long term and on the intermediate term. Figure 1.22 illustrates what I consider to be the last important cycle lows and highs as well as previous lows and highs. This information should assist you in updating your charts. Furthermore, I am willing to provide these charts to you for a nominal cost if you contact my office (see Appendix 1). The next step is to project the future low and high of the current cycle. This projection is easily accomplished by simply marking a dashed line to show the ideal cycle based on the average cycle length. In elementary terms, one simply locates the last low and projects forward in time the average cycle length showing the top as one-half the distance in time of the ideal cycle. Figure 7.2 shows how this would be done for a market with a cycle of four years average length. Figure 7.3 shows how this procedure is followed using the gold market as an example. It is important in this respect to differentiate between an ideal forecast and a price or trend expectation. It *must always* be remembered that forecasting the ideal cycle does not necessarily mean that the market will actually conform to the high and low projection that has been set forward as the ideal cycle. If this were the case, the markets would move up

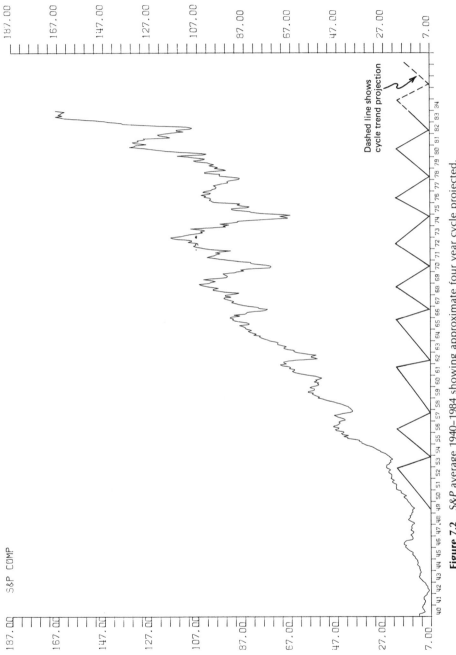

Figure 7.2 *S&P* average 1940–1984 showing approximate four year cycle projected. (Reprinted with permission of MBH Commodity Advisors, Inc., P.O. Box 353, Winnetka, IL 60093.)

S&P COMP

Dashed line shows cycle trend projection

97

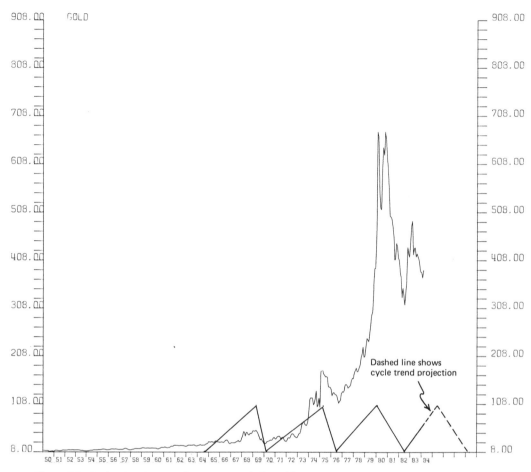

Figure 7.3 Projecting the next long-term cycle in gold.
(Reprinted with permission of MBH Commodity Advisors, Inc., P.O. Box 353, Winnetka, IL 60093.)

and down in regular waves, topping at the exact midpoint, and there would be no variation from one cycle to the next. Because this is not the case, the good market analyst/investor remembers that *a forecast is not a reality.* Forecasts must, in many cases, be adjusted to fit reality once reality is known. The projection serves merely as a guideline for accumulation and liquidation of positions in conjunction with the timing signals that have been and will continue to be proposed in this text. The purpose of projecting trends, including cycle top and cycle bottom, is first and foremost to serve as a plan of attack that will enable us to implement the moving average signals as well as the other confirmatory signals of a cyclic low or high. After the projection has been made, it is not changed unless a significant change occurs in the real time bottom that immediately preceded our projection. In other words, the cyclic projection will serve as our guideline of expectation, and we will apply the timing indicators and confirming indicators within the cyclic trend framework.

STEP 2: ENTER CYCLES ON YOUR LONG-TERM CHARTS

This is discussed in Chapter 4.

STEP 3: EVALUATE CURRENT POSITION OF CYCLES

If cycle is in appropriate time window for a turn, go to step 4. If not, wait until time is in phase for cyclic turn.

STEP 4: DETERMINE OPTIMUM MOVING AVERAGE

The next important step in the overall approach is to determine the moving average lengths for the given markets being analyzed. Figure 6.8 shows the moving averages I have found to be optimum for the individual markets based on my work with the cycles to this point in time. You can well appreciate the fact that no market text or analytical method is timeless, nor does any technique always serve the investor well. It is a matter of fact in the marketplace that things frequently change and as prices continue their movement, both the cycle lengths and the moving averages used as part of the overall strategy change, sometimes significantly. Therefore, the serious investor should research the current status of any suggested cycle lengths and/or moving averages (oscillators) discussed in this text. This procedure is, of course, in your best interest, and it is also consistent with my firm belief that every investor must do his or her own work and, in particular, his or her own updates. I believe that I have adequately stated my case for market update and I cannot overemphasize the importance of keeping current to make the most out of this or any other technique.

The only suggestion I can make in terms of keeping current is that you research several different moving average lengths, as well as oscillator lengths (discussed later), to optimize the moving averages at any given point in time. I believe that the moving averages listed in Figure 6.8 should serve the purpose for a reasonable number of years.

STEP 5: DETERMINE OPTIMUM CONFIRMATORY MOVING AVERAGE

The procedure used to determine the confirming moving average lengths is essentially similar to the methodology described in Step 4 above. Both moving averages should be separated by at least a three month time lag or, if we are using weekly moving averages, by at least a six week time lag. To have two moving averages that resemble one another too closely will not serve the purpose of our program and could result in false signals.

STEP 6: WAIT FOR MOVING AVERAGE CROSSOVER

This step requires perhaps the greatest amount of patience and investor maturity. This is also the step that causes investors the greatest amount of impatience and insecurity. Perhaps the best way I can tell you to proceed is to compare the investor to the hunter. The hunter goes to a location where game is likely to be. In the same way, the investor pays attention to a market that he or she finds interesting and isolates a proper time frame for a low or a high according to the guidelines presented herein. The hunter camouflages him or herself and lies in wait with loaded gun ready to shoot the prey when the time is right. As the hunter waits for game to appear, he or she may hear the rustling of leaves, the noise of a bush or a twig, or perhaps the noise of other hunters. He or she must continue to wait, taking great care not to overreact, and he or she must be particularly careful not to shoot too soon. To shoot at the wrong prey could mean serious trouble since it may be another hunter or perhaps one's own foot. Furthermore, to make excessive noise may mean that the hunted animal will be scared away and may not return. Although it is certainly impossible to scare the market away, it most certainly is possible to shoot too soon, thereby squandering needed ammunition (capital) and frustrating the hunter. If false signals are taken or if the hunter shoots too often at anything that moves, the result will most surely be a frustrated hunter with no ammunition. I am most certain that you can appreciate the analogies presented here and that you will profit by controlling your impatience and by acting only when the time is right.

Figure 7.4 presents in diagram form precisely the combination of moving average crossovers for which we are waiting. I make one assumption: that is, the market has entered the proper time frame for a low or a high. In order to do this, one simply calculates plus or minus 15% of the cycle length. For example, assume that the gold cycle is 6 years in length. Fifteen percent of 6 years equals .9 years. In turn, .9 years equals approximately 11 months. Ideally, then, the 11 month figure means, essentially, that prices in this market can bottom over an 11 month period plus or minus the length of the cycle. Figure 7.5 shows, ideally, how this is calculated. You can well appreciate the fact that 11 months plus or minus is a considerable period of time. In fact, it covers a 22 month period, which is almost two years. At this point, you may be asking yourself, "What good is the cycle?" Indeed, if the cycle had been the only criterion on which to judge the bottom of a market, it may well turn out to be invalid. Nonetheless, the entire purpose behind having timing indicators is to refine the length of the cycle. In addition, certain decisions (discussed later) will be made, based on the intermediate cycles that comprise the long-term cycles. First things first, however. Now that we have isolated the time window of the cyclic move on the long-term cycle, let us move to the next step to determine with greater accuracy the time window of the cyclic low. Previously, I mentioned the importance of the approximately 9–12 month cycle in the metals. Figure 7.6 shows how this cycles appears in recent history. You can appreciate the fact that this cycle is also asymmetrical and that prices tend to show different cycle lengths throughout time, although they do indeed cluster around an average cycle length of the given time frame. The next step, then, is to correlate the current

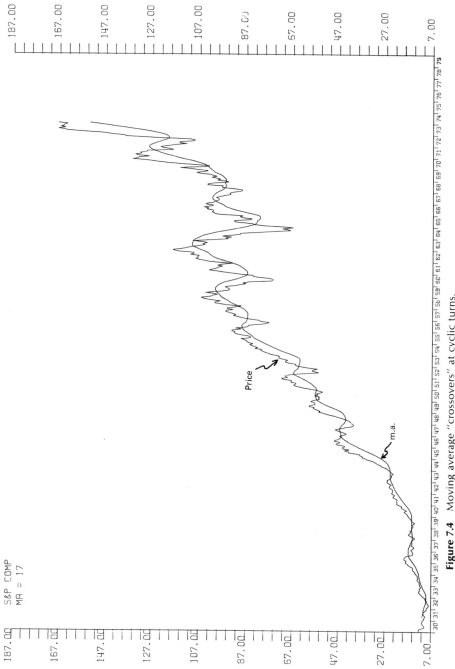

Figure 7.4 Moving average "crossovers" at cyclic turns.
(Reprinted with permission of MBH Commodity Advisors, Inc., P.O. Box 353, Winnetka, IL 60093.)

S&P COMP
MA = 17

Price

m.a.

101

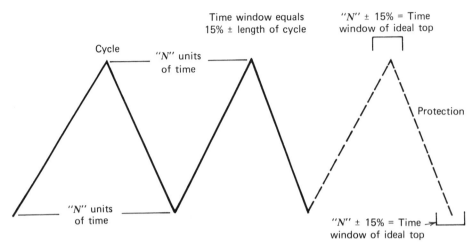

Figure 7.5 Calculation of 15 percent cycle deviation to yield "time window."

market situation on the long-term cycle with the intermediate-term cycle. This correlation is done simply by finding the last intermediate-term cycle low and projecting forward in time on the intermediate-term cycle to narrow down the time frame of the long-term cycle low. After this is done, the ideal cycle low can be determined with greater accuracy, thereby narrowing down the plus or minus 11 month time frame previously discussed as the plus or minus 15% degree of error for long-term cycles. The main consideration is, of course, that you understand precisely the procedure that is being used; consequently, I have chosen to illustrate extensively this phase of the procedure. Shown in Figures 7.7, 7.8, and 7.9 are the specific methods and procedures taken from my own charts showing both my market work and notes about the cycles. Nothing can replace practice, thus, I urge you to practice this phase because it is important to learn how this procedure works. It will not be necessary for you to spend an inordinately large amount of time on this step, but it will be necessary for you to gain a considerable degree of facility in the methodology that comprises this aspect of the proposed decision-making process.

Remember, however, that the intermediate-term cycle itself is also a function of degree of error and that 15% plus or minus an ideal 11 month cycle yields an error factor of plus or minus 1.7 months. I hope you can appreciate what has now been done with cycles. Essentially, we have started with a long-term cycle of 6 years, we have narrowed it down to an intermediate-term cycle of approximately 11 months, and we have narrowed down our potential degree of error to 1.7 months. *This does not mean that we will hit the exact top or bottom of any market plus or minus 1.7 months.* All it means is that we have narrowed the time frame within which we will look for our timing signals to confirm a bottom. It is entirely possible that the market will bottom or top much earlier or later than expected. Techniques for coping with such situations, however, will be discussed in the further suggestions explained later in this chapter. You will observe, by the way, that few of the examples illustrated in this text are hypothetical. I have attempted to restrict my work to real mar-

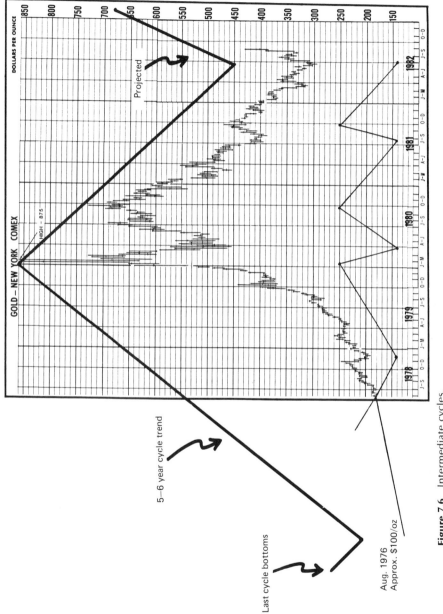

Figure 7.6 Intermediate cycles.
(Reprinted with permission of Commodity Research Bureau, 75 Montgomery St., Jersey City, NJ 07302.)

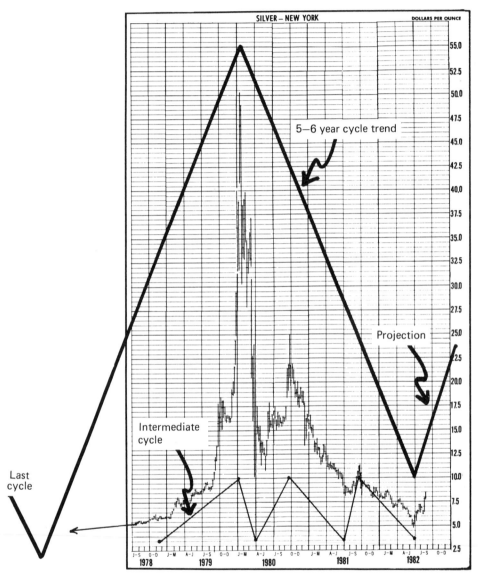

Figure 7.7 Projecting cycles.
(Reprinted with permission of Commodity Research Bureau, 75 Montgomery St., Jersey City, NJ 07302.)

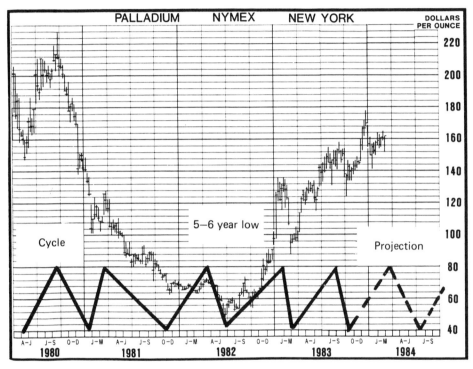

Figure 7.8 Projecting cycles.
(Reprinted with permission of Commodity Research Bureau, 75 Montgomery St., Jersey City, NJ 07302.)

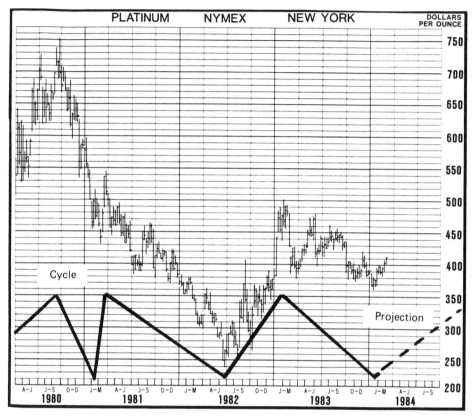

Figure 7.9 Projecting cycles.
(Reprinted with permission of Commodity Research Bureau, 75 Montgomery St., Jersey City, NJ 07302.)

ket history and real market situations to show you that my theory of cyclic investing is reasonably applied to the history of precious metals cycles.

STEP 7: TAKING ACTION

Now our procedure becomes quite simple and easily implemented. Using our long-term and intermediate-term cycle charts, we begin to look for a cross of moving average over price for market bottoms, direction of moving average, and at tops the opposite. Figure 7.10 is a three-paneled example of a given market prior to crossing over its moving average, in the process of crossing over its moving average, and several months after crossing over its moving average. Determination of the crossover is an objective procedure and ordinarily not subject to interpetation. Figure 7.11 shows how the primary and confirmatory moving averages function in respect to market tops and market bottoms with the primary rule being the need for price to cross over both moving averages *and* for both moving averages to be heading in the same direction. It is impor-

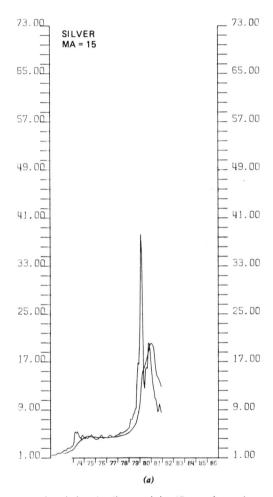

Figure 7.10 a Three stages of cycle low in silver and the 15 month moving average of silver prices. (Reprinted with permission of MBH Commodity Advisors, Inc., P.O. Box 353, Winnetka, IL 60093.)

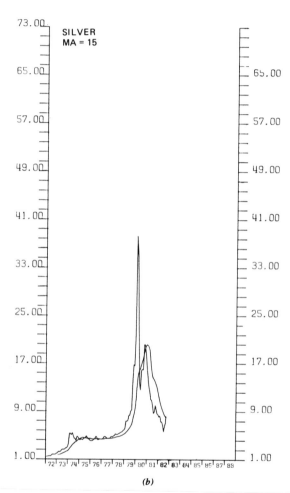

Figure 7.10 b Three stages of cycle low in silver and the 15 month moving average of silver prices. (Reprinted with permission of MBH Commodity Advisors, Inc., P.O. Box 353, Winnetka, IL 60093.)

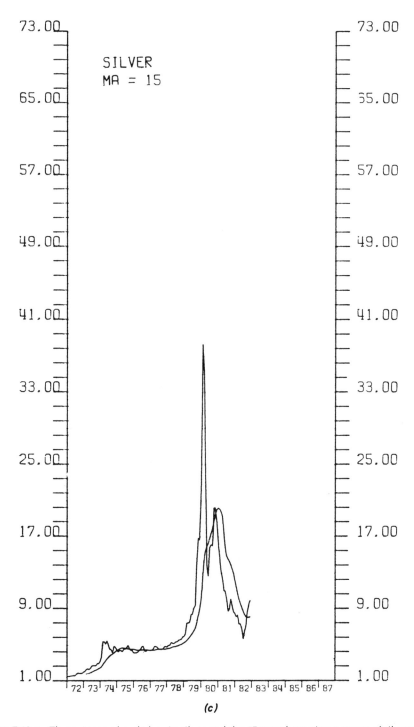

Figure 7.10 c   Three stages of cycle low in silver and the 15 month moving average of silver prices. (Reprinted with permission of MBH Commodity Advisors, Inc., P.O. Box 353, Winnetka, IL 60093.)

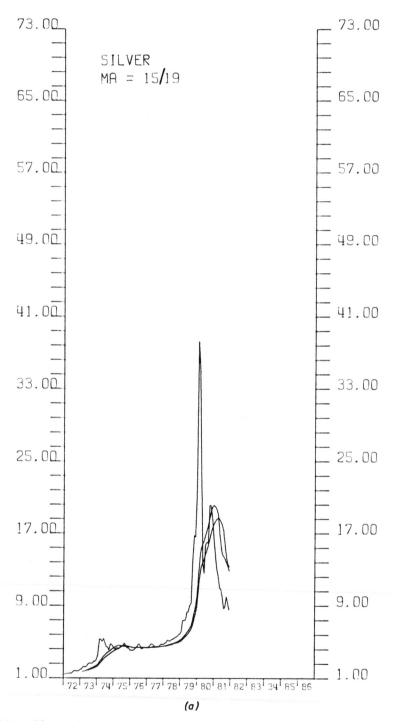

Figure 7.11 a Silver and 15 month plus 19 month moving average confirming turns.
(Reprinted with permission of MBH Commodity Advisors, Inc., P.O. Box 353, Winnetka, IL 60093.)

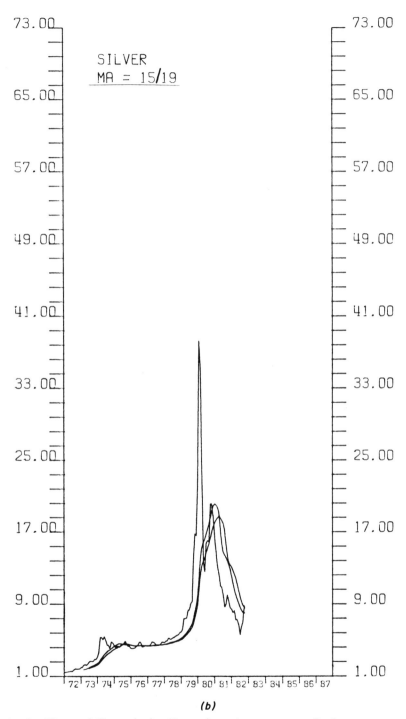

Figure 7.11 b Silver and 15 month plus 19 month moving average confirming turns.
(Reprinted with permission of MBH Commodity Advisors, Inc., P.O. Box 353, Winnetka, IL 60093.)

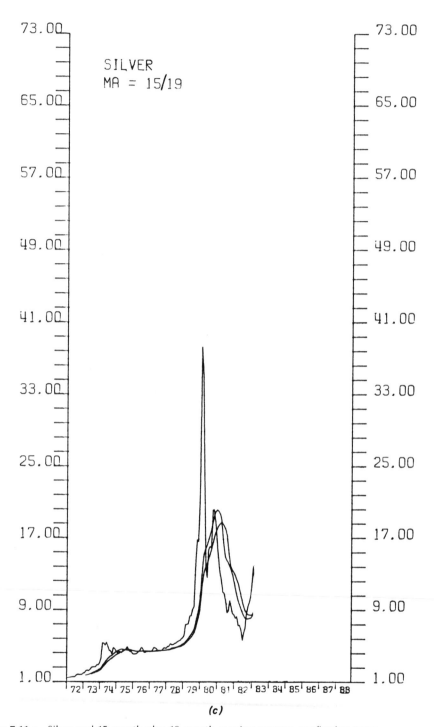

Figure 7.11 c Silver and 15 month plus 19 month moving average confirming turns.
(Reprinted with permission of MBH Commodity Advisors, Inc., P.O. Box 353, Winnetka, IL 60093.)

112

tant that both moving averages be heading in the same direction since it is the job of the confirmatory moving average to validate the change in cycles and the up or down trend.

The confirmatory moving average is always the longer of the two moving averages you have selected. Price will first cross over the shorter of the two moving averages, and it will then cross over the confirmatory moving average, thereby validating the change in trend. If this chain of events occurs within the appropriate cyclic time window, our ideal signal will have been triggered, and we may then proceed to shoot with both barrels. In other words, our buying program can begin. This is the ideal situation. But since I am cognizant of the fact that nothing always works in its ideal form, the astute investor will begin his or her accumulation progam prior to the market bottom, and his or her liquidation program prior to the ideal top. My suggestion, therefore, is to begin accumulating twice the time length ahead of and after the percentage variation on the intermediate-term cycle. In essence, the ideal cycle is 11 months. In the ideal cycle, 15% equals 1.7 months. Twice 1.7 months equals 3.4 months. Rounding off 3.4 months, I arrive at 3 months. Therefore, based on the empirical evidence in gold and silver prices, I recommend beginning an accumulation program in metals approximately 3 months ahead of the ideal projected low and continuing approximately 3 months beyond the ideal projected low. The ideal projected low must, of course, be a function of both the intermediate and long-term cycles. The specific quantities that should be bought ahead of the projected low and beyond the projected low will be outlined in Chapter 10. As a general rule, however, I recommend 10% accumulation of final intended amount per month until after the low has been confirmed by the indicators presented here. After the low has been confirmed, approximatley 30% more can be invested, leaving a 20% cash reserve. The remaining 20% should, based on my analysis, be held back for the purpose of meeting unforeseen obligations and/or margin on the contracts currently being held. Remember that the only time accumulation or scale out selling of longs occurs during the intermediate term cycle is when the long term cycles are in phase for lows or highs.

8

Review of Suggested Methods and Procedures

I realize that you have just been given a considerable amount of material and that a review of the recommended methods and procedures might be helpful. This chapter, therefore, is designed as a checklist to assist you in your decision-making process. I would suggest you keep your own checklist sheet for each market.

1. The metals markets have long-term and intermediate-term cycles.
2. The approximate average cycle lengths for each market have been given.
3. By starting at the last cycle low or cycle high, one can project the next time window or ideal turning period for the coming high or low.
4. After the ideal time frame of the next low or high has been projected, go to the *intermediate-term cycle* for the given market and project its coming low or high to obtain an approximate time frame of the cycle low or high.
5. After the ideal time frame has been entered, it is time to begin looking for confirming indicators. These indicators can take the form of any or all of the following:

   a. Monthly up-side or down-side price reversal.
   b. Monthly *low/high* or *high/low* close.
   c. *Combination* of *a* and *b*.
   d. *Penetration of resistance or support* level as illustrated. It should be noted that market tops tend to form quickly and a support level is

rarely established. Cycle lows, on the other hand, tend to take more time to form and usually form resistance levels.

e. *Moving averages* are then watched as additional confirmatory indicators. It is preferable to use the double moving average indicator as an idex of when the market has made a long term cycle or high.

f. *Oscillators* as described are also used to confirm an *oversold* condition that usually comes at market bottoms or an *overbought* condition that usually comes at market tops.

g. *Bullish consensus* or contrary opinion indicators also are helpful in evaluating the existing sentiment. If it is excessively negative, then the market is probably at a low point, whereas an excessively bullish reading suggests that a top is forming.

6. Naturally one would feel more certain of a turn in the market if the confluence of confirmatory indicators is substantial. The more confirmation we can receive in the way of timing signals, the better the top or bottom is likely to be.

7. The specific procedure for establishing positions is, to a certain extent, a function of the individual investor's financial ability. At the end of this chapter I outline several strategies depending on your specific financial ability. Remember, however, that long-term investment in metals or, for that matter in any market requires persistence and the ability to overlook short-term emotion, price fluctuation, news, and opinions. The greatest shortcoming of many investors is that they react too quickly to exit a position either after a small, quick profit has been made or when they show a quick loss. The long-term program stresses accumulation at or within bottoming areas, and liquidation at or within top areas.

8. The long-term investor must, therefore, set aside a given amount of capital that he or she is willing to risk as part of the program. In some cases an investor will be more suited to a program of cash market accumulation, whereas other investors will be interested in higher leverage such as that found in futures or options. Still other investors will be interested in buying or selling shares of stock in mining companies. All of these approaches are acceptable. Chapter 10 discusses the portfolio and money management considerations of this program.

BUYING AND SELLING ON A SCALE IN AND SCALE OUT

I previously mentioned the desirability of accumulating metals (in their various forms) on a *scale-in* basis when the cycles were in a bottoming phase. I also indicated that liquidation on a *scale-out* basis was the way to exit positions at or near a cyclic top. The accumulation process is usually a longer one than is the liquidation process because markets tend to bottom slowly and top quickly.

In view of this I suggest the following basic approach for establishing a long-term position in the metals:

1. Begin by taking a 15% of total available funds position in metals as the ideal time frame of the low is entered. More conservative investors can establish an initial position after the first timing signal has been seen, but they will probably pay more for their metals if they wait until then.

2. After the market is midway through the ideal time window (i.e., half of the computed time window length) a second 15% position can be taken. Now you are 30% invested and should be close to the bottom of average price. More conservative investors can wait for a second timing signal, if desired; however, there are cases in which only two timing signals will appear.

3. The next 15% should be taken when resistance has been penetrated. This brings the total to 45%.

4. The next 15% should be taken when prices have penetrated their double moving averages. This brings the total to 60% investment. At this point prices should be well on their way. In some cases the lows are "tested" and the double moving averages are again penetrated to the down side. This has recently happened in silver. In such an event, the balance of funds held in reserve (40%) will be placed into play. By this I mean that when the double moving averages are again penetrated to the up side, another 15% will be taken out of reserve and placed into the long side bringing the total position to 75%.

5. I am generally opposed to a full 100% position on either the long side or the short side. Therefore, in keeping with my generally conservative approach, the remaining 25% is held in reserve. In general, the long-term approach is based on the old concept of "dollar cost averaging." The only thing standing between the investor and profits is patience and time.

6. I am also opposed to "pyramiding" positions (i.e., adding additional positions on the basis of open profits) since this tends to raise one's cost, thereby defeating the ultimate purpose of dollar cost averaging.

NOW LET US LOOK AT EXITING THE MARKET

I have indicated several times that exiting a position requires more speed and sales in larger quantity since tops tend to be violent and swift. It is, therefore, much easier to enter at or near lows than it is to exit at or near highs. The world is full of investors with defeatist attitudes because of their inability to exit at the precise top. My feeling is that to take out 60% of a major bull move is to have achieved a great deal more than many investors do. To come within 20% of the top or the bottom is, therefore, admirable considering what happens in reality to most investors. In looking at the manner in which to exit a long-term position in metals, it is important to consider the previously mentioned fact that tops tend to be "fast and furious." Notwithstanding the fact that tops can arrive late in the cycle, I always opt for safety and I, therefore, suggest selling out 20% of the position within the time frame of the ideal top. I stress that the important consideration is *time* and not *price*. Cycles look primarily at time and not primarily at price.

In exiting 20% of the long position you will be left with 55% of your available capital invested. Thirty percent should be sold as soon as a timing signal has been spotted. Hence, the remaining position is 25% of available capital. This amount should be liquidated as soon as the double moving averages have been taken out on the down side. Less conservative investors can fine tune these procedures to suit their individual needs and abilities. I am certain that you can see my penchant for conservatism. More aggressive traders, for example, can sell short or buy put options.

IF THE "UNEXPECTED" HAPPENS

As an investor you know that the unexpected is always a possibility. Assume, for example, that a cycle tops early after giving signals to buy. Naturally you know that this will happen at times and that *there is always risk and the probability of being wrong*. My rule of thumb is this: In entering a long position that goes in your favor but peaks early, liquidate the entire position if new lows are made after the market is more than 30% of the time length into its projected cycle up trend. In other words, a cycle may top early (this usually happens in a deflationary economy). To protect yourself, you should close out your long position when the lows of the cycle are broken after the cycle has run 30% of its length (for example, a six year cycle should have run about two years from its low point). Finally, as a general word of caution that is applicable in all investments, "When in doubt, stay out." In other words, if you cannot figure out a cycle, a time length, or a signal, then stay out of the market until you can figure things out. (Though I do not have all the answers, I am available and I do study the markets intensively. Therefore, if you have a brief question, I will try and answer it if you drop me a line.)

9

Seasonal Factors in Metals

The effect of seasonal movement in precious metals prices is as significant as it is in virtually all the commodity markets. The term *seasonality* has been used for many years, although it is often not understood by the individuals who use it most frequently. Many investors and market analysts employ a rigid interpretation of seasonals and labor under the misperception that seasonal patterns are general forecasts of price trends during given periods of the year. W. D. Gann, who was perhaps the first to use seasonality in futures trading, was quite clear in his definition.* Specifically, Mr. Gann felt that prices, particularly in agricultural commodities, usually follow certain market patterns, topping and bottoming within reasonably close time frames each calendar year. Before detailing the specific uses of seasonal factors, let us first examine my understanding of seasonals and the manner in which I recommend they be used.

The use of seasonality in the commodity markets is not a new concept. During the 1970s and 80s a number of books and studies dealing with the technique have been published. In 1977, MBH released *Seasonal Chart Study 1953-1977—Cash Commodities*. This study was one of the first serious attempts to quantify seasonals in the commodity markets. In 1979, MBH published *Seasonal Chart Study II—Commodity Spreads*. This report provided a week by week seasonal analysis of commodity spreads and isolated many highly reliable trends in a number of markets. Williams and Noseworthy, in their *Sure Thing Commodity Trading,* provided speculators with a list of specific seasonal trades having high reliabilities during the past ten years or so.† This study was a pioneering effort in the isolation of specific seasonal trades in the futures market, on a market by market basis.

---

* W. D. Gann, *How to Make Profits in Commodities.* (Pomeroy, WA: Lambert-Gann, 1943.)
† L. Williams, and M. Noseworthy, *Sure Thing Commodity Trading* (Brightwaters, NY: Windsor, 1977).

The combined effect of these and other efforts has been to increase markedly the use of seasonals. It is unfortunate that, despite all the available information, few traders can use seasonal concepts to their advantage. Too often, speculators will seek to justify an already established position by referring to seasonals. If the seasonal does not agree with their opinion, they will ignore the seasonal. If there is agreement, they may then double up on the position. Moreover, some traders understand the concept of seasonality and are aware of key seasonal trades, however, they do not have the patience to trade them effectively.

W. D. Gann underscored the importance of seasonality in commodity futures prices. His book *How to Make Profits in Commodities* devotes considerable time and space to this concept. Today, with the assistance of computer technology, it is possible to determine accurately and specifically most seasonal trends in the commodity futures markets. Whereas Gann was primarily interested in using seasonal highs and lows, my study of seasonality was an effort to fill the void in short-term data. The lack of such information has left many traders uncertain about the usual yearly pattern in each market. It is difficult to believe that even today many traders to not know what seasonals for each market are, nor do they believe in their importance.

WHAT IS A SEASONAL?

Commodity markets move in fairly regular price patterns. To most traders these cyclical movements are neither obvious nor meaningful, which is unfortunate since regularity and repetition are the cornerstones of profitable trading. All trading systems seek to isolate signals or indicators that repeat themselves frequently enough and reliably enough to permit profitable trading. Seasonals and cycles are the ultimate factors underlying market regularity. Anyone who has read my 1978 study, *Commodities—Now Through 1984,* should be familiar with the underlying long-range cycles in each market.* Although a few of the specific forecasts I made have not yet come to pass, the more radical expectations have indeed become reality in the last year, which attests to the validity of cycles. Within the cyclical patterns we find shorter-term repetitions in price trends, including seasonals.

The price of virtually every commodity is affected by weather, season, and growing conditions. Supply and demand are also a function of seasonal fluctuations. When crops are large, after a harvest, it would be natural to assume that prices may be lower due to farmer selling. When demand for feed grains is high, during winter months, we might expect prices to be higher. Certainly all factors, if known, would permit the errorless forecasting of prices. The markets themselves are perfect, I maintain. It is our ability to recognize and use all of the price inputs that is imperfect. Hence, our forecasting ability is limited. Since seasonal factors affect prices, it is possible, or should be possible, to determine if and when a given market will move up or down due to seasonality. A seasonal pattern is, therefore, the tendency of a given cash or futures market to

* Jacob Bernstein, *Commodities—Now Through 1984* (Winnetka, IL: MBH, 1979).

trend in a given direction at certain times of the year. We do not always know the reasons for seasonal price movements. Personally, I do not need to know why a market moves up or down at a given time of the year. Certainly, knowing "why" makes some traders more secure. My concern is not with the *why* of things but rather with the *that* of things. I do not know why a given market moves up 90% of the time during November, but I do know *that* it makes the move. My security comes from the profit I can reap by having this knowledge. "Ours is not a reason why, ours is but to sell and buy." Figures 9.1 through 9.4 illustrate and explain the seasonal price patterns that have been prevalent in several of the cash metals markets dating back many years.

SEASONAL FACTORS IN THE FUTURES MARKETS

In addition to the previously explained seasonal tendency in cash metals (and most other commodity markets), there are several definite seasonal price tendencies in the futures markets. The seasonal tendencies reflect many of the

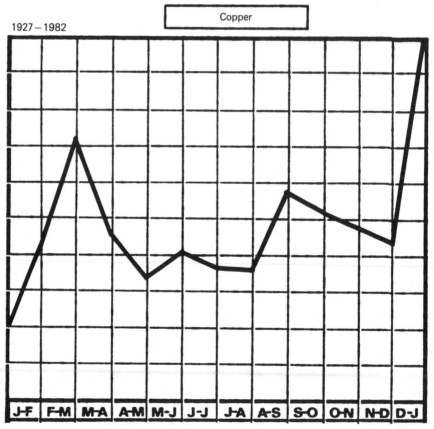

Figure 9.1   Cash copper seasonal pattern.
(Reprinted with permission of MBH Commodity Advisors, Inc., P.O. Box 353, Winnetka, IL 60093.)

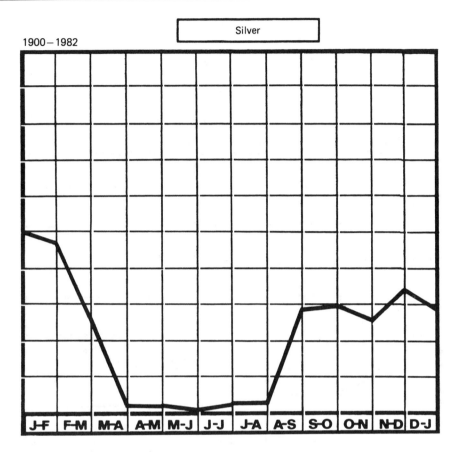

Figure 9.2 Cash silver seasonal pattern.
(Reprinted with permission of MBH Commodity Advisors, Inc., P.O. Box 353, Winnetka, IL 60093.)

patterns seen in cash metals; however, some seasonal movements have been unique to futures during the last 10–20 years. To understand the fashion in which futures seasonals may be used in the metals markets, it is first necessary to understand the manner in which they are derived. The basis for this research appeared in my publication *Seasonal Futures Charts.** In effect, the futures seasonals are derived through the use of a computerized system that analyzes futures data on a weekly basis. My ongoing research has shown that there are distinct weekly seasonal patterns in metal futures as well as in virtually all other futures. Not every week of the year has a seasonal tendency, but certain weeks stand out as significant time frames during which a high probability of movement in a given direction can be expected.

* Jacob Bernstein, *Seasonal Futures Charts* (Winnetka, IL.: MBH, 1984).

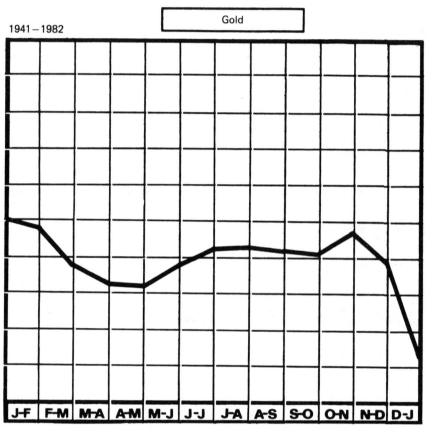

1941–1982

Gold

J-F F-M M-A A-M M-J J-J J-A A-S S-O O-N N-D D-J

Figure 9.3 Cash gold seasonal pattern.
(Reprinted with permission of MBH Commodity Advisors, Inc., P.O. Box 353, Winnetka, IL 60093.)

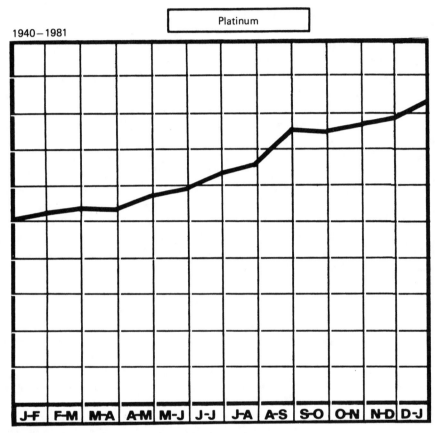

1940 – 1981

Platinum

Figure 9.4 Cash platinum seasonal pattern.
(Reprinted with permission of MBH Commodity Advisors, Inc., P.O. Box 353, Winnetka, IL 60093.)

A FEW NECESSARY DETAILS

To understand fully the futures seasonal concept you must first understand how the data is derived. This understanding requires only a small degree of mathematical knowledge. Fortunately, the computer has now made it possible for all of us to be mathematical "wizards," doing voluminous research for us while we find more and better ways to spend our potential profits. The basic approach is depicted in flow chart fashion (Fig. 9.5). In effect, a given futures delivery month is studied on a year to year basis across the available data history. Each week is seen as a unique entity, and price changes from the previous weekly close is calculated. All the price changes for the given week are then compared, both in magnitude and direction. An index is then computed showing average magnitude of change and direction (i.e., percent of time up from previous weekly closing price). The price magnitude index reading is then added to the previous weekly plot, and a cumulative plot is charted with a "percent of time up" reading shown in the weekly block below it.

For anyone who wants to perform this work on their own computer systems the basic steps are outlined below. For anyone who wants a more specific breakdown on the technique, including the plotting software, Appendix II lists the Fortran IV program I have been using to accomplish the given results. Figures 9.6 through 9.13 show the seasonal futures patterns for several contract months in the metals. Although these patterns will change as time goes by, they are likely to change in the direction of more reliability as opposed to less reliability.

Now that we have examined the traditional interpretations and suggested

HOW THE SEASONALS WERE DETERMINED

It is not necessary to have a background in computer programming to understand the manner in which this study was prepared. In order for you to more fully appreciate the results, and the amount of work which went into their production, I suggest you familiarize yourself with the methodology. Here, in step form, is the procedure which we followed in our computer analysis.

Take the daily history file for a given market and month, for each year on file, ie. June Live Cattle '67, '68, '69, '70...   Read this data from tape to a disk file.

Line up each contract by date. The last day of trading is treated as day 1, the second of last day as day 2 etc. This is done since not all contracts terminate on the same precise calendar day. There are specific rules for determining last day of trading as set by the exchange, however, and most contracts will terminate on or about the same week.

Calculate the price change for each week using the Friday price as the last price, or the Thursday price if Friday was not a trading day. In so doing we end up with a weekly price change for each market and year.

Standardize or normalize the price changes for each year. This is done to limit the effect of unusually wide or unusually small price swings. We are primarily interested in direction of move, or trend from one week to the next.

Once data has been normalized take the algebraic average for each column of week. This yields an index of average weekly fluctuation per week of the year.

Determine the percentage of years during which price was up or down for given week.

Dump data to plotter and plot cumulative price trend line.

Figure 9.5 Computer procedure for determining futures seasonal tendencies.

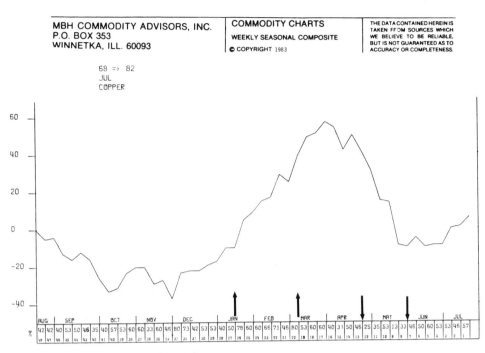

Figure 9.6 Seasonal futures chart, July, copper.
(Reprinted with permission of MBH Commodity Advisors, Inc., P.O. Box 353, Winnetka, IL 60093.)

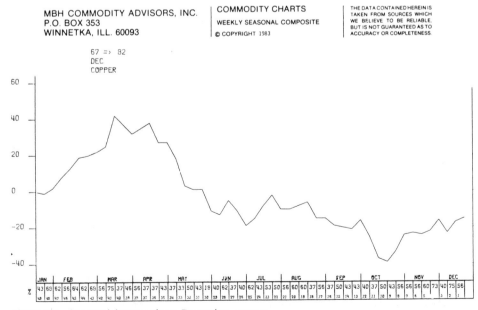

Figure 9.7 Seasonal futures chart, December, copper.
(Reprinted with permission of MBH Commodity Advisors, Inc., P.O. Box 353, Winnetka, IL 60093.)

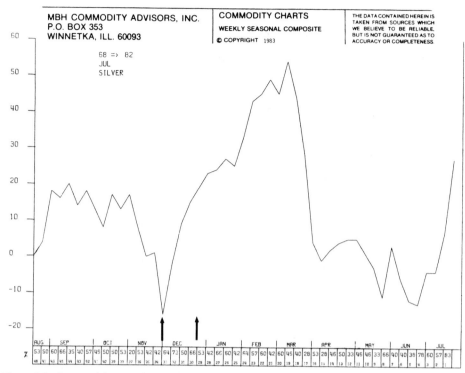

Figure 9.8 Seasonal futures chart, July, silver.
(Reprinted with permission of MBH Commodity Advisors, Inc., P.O. Box 353, Winnetka, IL 60093.)

Figure 9.9 Seasonal futures chart, December, silver.
(Reprinted with permission of MBH Commodity Advisors, Inc., P.O. Box 353, Winnetka, IL 60093.)

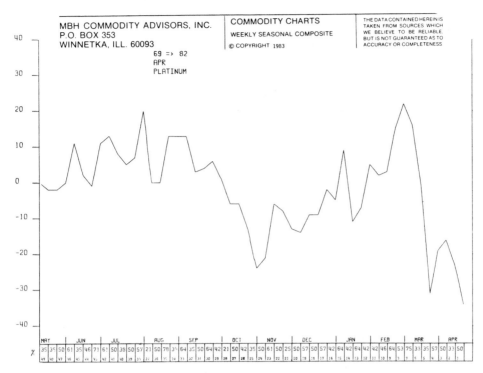

Figure 9.10 Seasonal futures chart, April, platinum.
(Reprinted with permission of MBH Commodity Advisors, Inc., P.O. Box 353, Winnetka, IL 60093.)

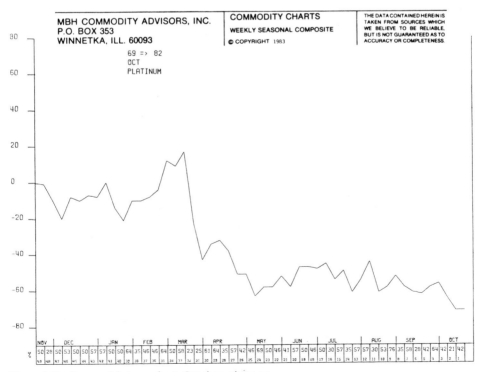

Figure 9.11 Seasonal futures chart, October, platinum.
(Reprinted with permission of MBH Commodity Advisors, Inc., P.O. Box 353, Winnetka, IL 60093.)

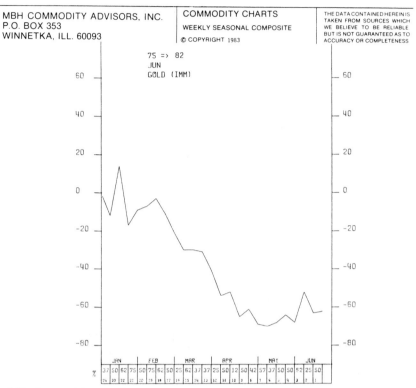

Figure 9.12 Seasonal futures chart, June, gold.
(Reprinted with permission of MBH Commodity Advisors, Inc., P.O. Box 353, Winnetka, IL 60093.)

Figure 9.13 Seasonal futures chart, December, gold.
(Reprinted with permission of MBH Commodity Advisors, Inc., P.O. Box 353, Winnetka, IL 60093.)

uses for seasonals, I will become more specific regarding seasonal methods I have recently researched.

CRITICAL SEASONAL MONTHS

I have maintained for a long time that every market has its own seasonal personality; in essence, prices *should* do certain things at certain times of the year. Conversely, if a market does not do what it should do at a given time of the year, I suspect that a move in the opposite direction is quite likely. Certain months, for example, appear to be critically important in price patterns and trends. Perhaps the best illustration I can give you about critical seasonal months is my "elevator analogy." When you are on an elevator heading for the fourteenth floor, it is impossible to travel to your fourteenth floor destination without first passing through all stories below the fourteenth. This is a simple concept, and I believe it applies to the markets as well.

I would like to illustrate for you the concept of critical seasonal month as it applies to the futures market in pork bellies. Assume for a moment that I gave you the following general rules: (1) "Buy the February pork belly futures if they close above the highest high they made during the month of May," and (2) "Sell February pork belly futures if they close below the lowest low they made during the month of June." The concept is simple enough, but it does require further clarification. First, what do I mean by the highest high? Specifically, I mean the highest intraday price high during the entire month of May and, conversely, the lowest low is the lowest price low during the entire month of June. The next point relates to exactly when and for how long the rules apply. The rules begin to apply as soon as trading for the critical calendar month has been completed. Therefore, after May is over, the test for the "penetration of May high rule" is in effect. It remains in effect up to and including the last day of the futures contract. Trading the futures contract into the delivery period, however, is not something recommended. In fact, the last day during which the rule could be implemented would be the last trading day of January. Essentially, the same basic consideration would hold true for the June rule except that it would go into effect as soon as the month of June has ended. It would continue until the same period of time as the May rule. Figures 9.14 through 9.19 illustrate quite clearly the point I am making. An examination of these figures will reveal that the critical month rule for pork belly futures can be a valuable aid to long-term profits, as long as it continues its high level of predictability. Remember, however, that nothing has been said about stop loss or degree of risk. Each individual trader must decide how he or she would like to evaluate risk. In general, however, a good rule of thumb in pork bellies is to risk back to the May high if selling short on the June critical month signal, or to the June low if buying on the June critical month signal. The critical month concept has considerable significance in agricultural commodities. For many years, however, I failed to investigate its applicability to metals, assuming, erroneously, that it would not be reliable. In recent years I have discovered that the critical month concept is one of my most valuable interpretive tools in the metals sector. *Remember*, therefore, that each market has its own critical months!

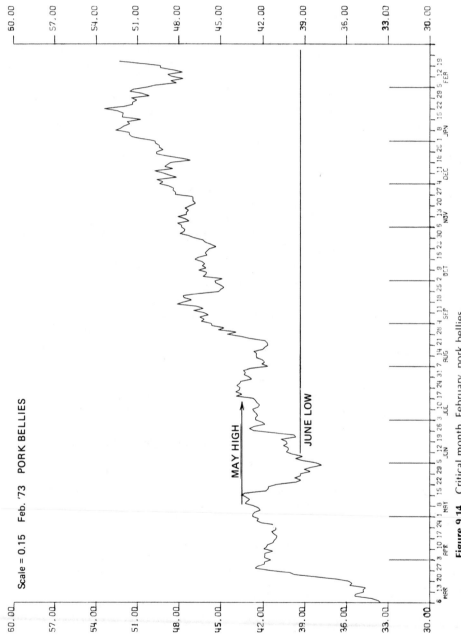

Figure 9.14 Critical month, February, pork bellies.
(Reprinted with permission of MBH Commodity Advisors, Inc., P.O. Box 353, Winnetka, IL 60093.)

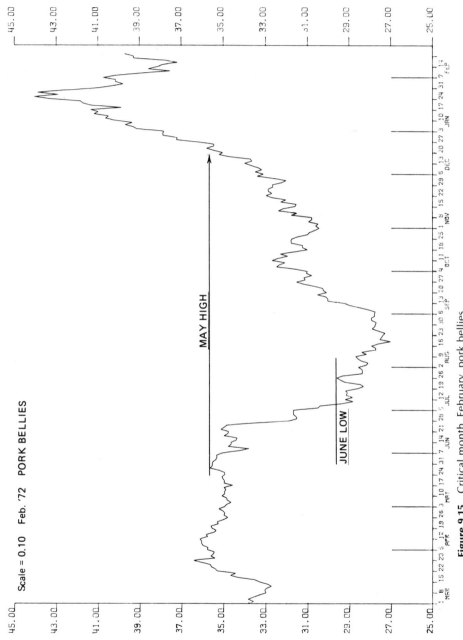

Figure 9.15 Critical month, February, pork bellies.
(Reprinted with permission of MBH Commodity Advisors, Inc., P.O. Box 353, Winnetka, IL 60093.)

131

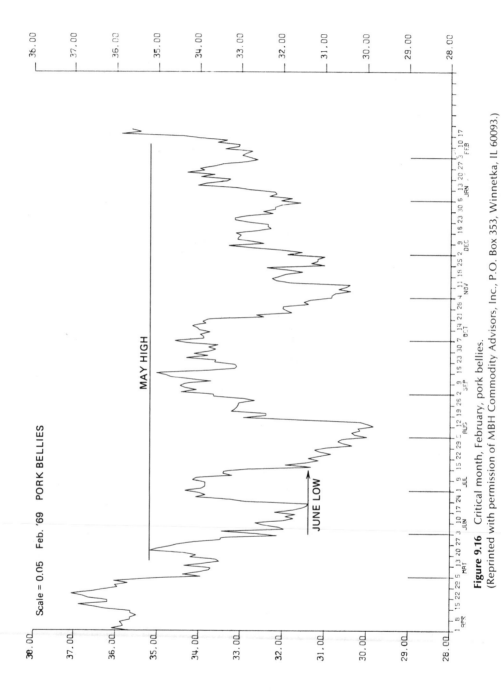

Figure 9.16 Critical month, February, pork bellies.
(Reprinted with permission of MBH Commodity Advisors, Inc., P.O. Box 353, Winnetka, IL 60093.)

132

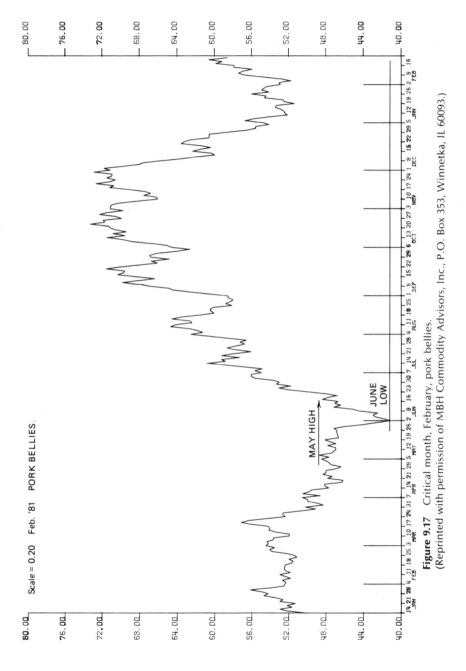

Figure 9.17 Critical month, February, pork bellies.
(Reprinted with permission of MBH Commodity Advisors, Inc., P.O. Box 353, Winnetka, IL 60093.)

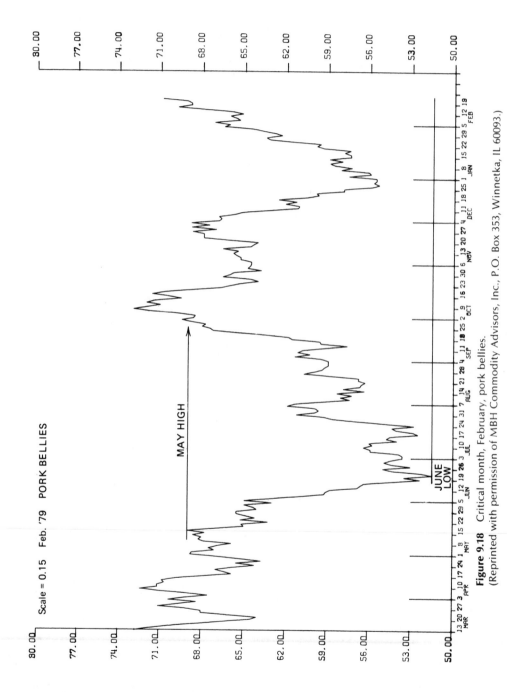

Figure 9.18 Critical month, February, pork bellies.
(Reprinted with permission of MBH Commodity Advisors, Inc., P.O. Box 353, Winnetka, IL 60093.)

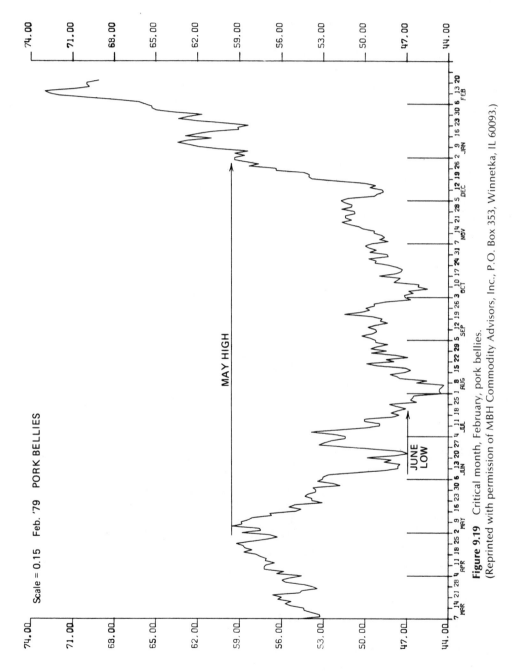

Figure 9.19 Critical month, February, pork bellies.
(Reprinted with permission of MBH Commodity Advisors, Inc., P.O. Box 353, Winnetka, IL 60093.)

135

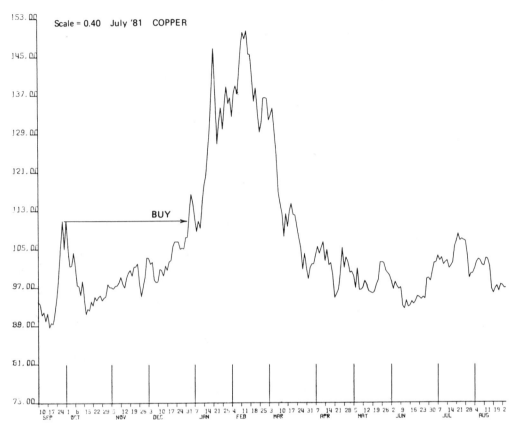

Figure 9.20 Critical month, July, copper futures.
(Reprinted with permission of MBH Commodity Advisors, Inc., P.O. Box 353, Winnetka, IL 60093.)

Critical Month in Copper

The critical month concept has important implications for analyzing and profitably trading copper futures. Its reliability has significance for the investor and speculator alike. Figures 9.20 through 9.25 show examples of the critical months for July copper futures. The brief synopsis in Figure 9.26 discusses critical month use in copper futures as well as the mechanics of how one might buy or sell based on the critical month.

Critical Month in Silver and Gold

Similarly, the critical month analogy is important in evaluating seasonal price patterns for gold and silver. Figures 9.27 through 9.31 illustrate the concept as it has applied to these markets. You can see that there are both bullish and bearish factors, each of which must be given sufficient attention during any contract year.

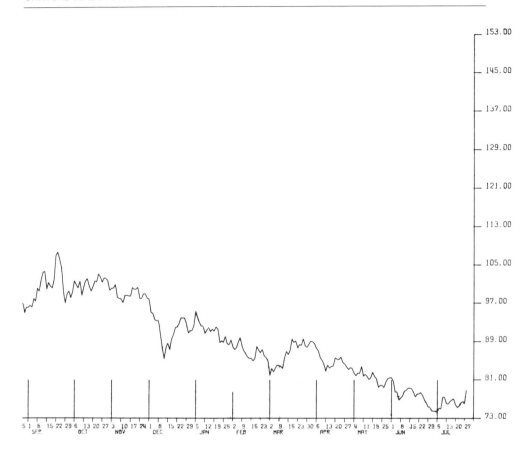

153.00

145.00

137.00

129.00

121.00

113.00

105.00

97.00

89.00

81.00

73.00

5 1 6 15 22 29 6 13 20 27 3 10 17 24 1 8 15 22 29 5 12 19 25 2 9 15 23 2 9 15 23 30 6 13 20 27 4 11 19 25 1 8 15 22 29 5 15 20 27
  SEP.   OCT   NOV   DEC   JAN   FEB   MAR   APR   MAY   JUN   JUL

Using Critical Months in the Investment Program

Because the critical month is such an important factor in evaluating precious metals' trends during any given year, the informed investor should always pay sufficient attention to critical months. This procedure is applicable to copper as well as to silver and gold. Moveover, it is considerably useful when one wishes to establish a position. How might this work? Assume that a long-term cycle in gold has bottomed and you wish to begin accumulating a position. Assume also that prices may be in a trading range for several months without establishing a definitive break-out to the up side. The wise investor could keep his or her funds on the sidelines, avoiding all purchases unless the critical month to the up side has been triggered, thereby indicating the probable start of an important move. During each successive phase of the cycle, the critical month could be used as a means by which additional units could be purchased.

By including seasonality in our approach to the metals, we have added a significant analytical aid to our long-term investment program. Through the use of seasonals, informed investors can determine how and when to enter the

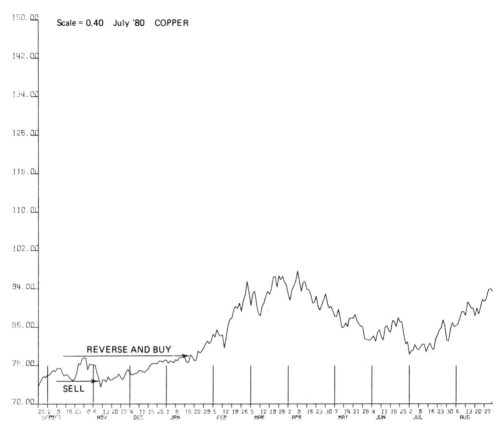

Figure 9.21   Critical month, July, copper futures.
(Reprinted with permission of MBH Commodity Advisors, Inc., P.O. Box 353, Winnetka, IL 60093.)

long side of a market. They can also determine how and when either to liquidate their position or to sell short if they are so inclined. Most important, the
critical months and other seasonal concepts work best when implemented in
conjunction with the long-term cycle trend. It is, therefore, preferable to use
critical month buy signals in conjunction with the upward phase of a given
long-term cycle, and critical month sell signals in conjunction with the downward phase of a critical month sell signal. In addition, remember that any given
market tool is only as good as the discipline of its user. The right tool in the
wrong hands can become a destructive weapon rather than an investment aid.

"KEY SEASONAL DATES" IN METAL FUTURES

The seasonal concept can be carried one step further by selecting certain
key data during the calendar year that have shown a marked tendency as
starting dates for up or down moves. You will recall that we first examined cash
monthly seasonal tendencies followed by weekly seasonal patterns in the fu-

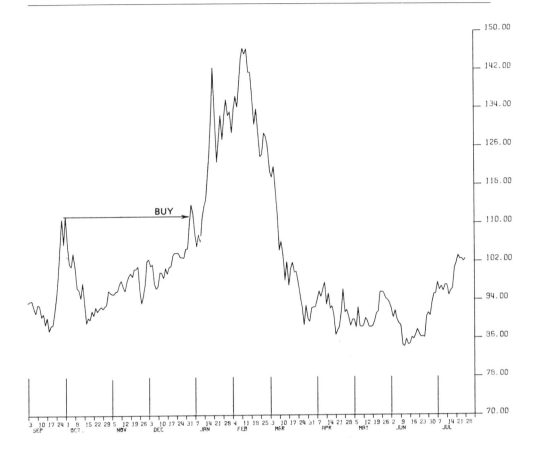

tures markets. Now we will go one step further and examine the markets from a more specific orientation.

What Is a "Key Seasonal Date"?

Early in this chapter I established the fact that prices in many markets tend to move in given patterns during the year. Though these patterns are not always similar, many tend to repeat themselves often enough to gain "cyclic" or repetitive status that could be demonstrated as statistically valid (i.e., greater than chance). In my work with seasonals and cycles I noticed that certain dates during most years were significant as either starting dates of up moves or down moves, whereas other dates usually marked the end of up moves and/or down moves. I termed these dates "key seasonal dates" because they marked important starting and ending points of price moves during *most* years. The word "most" is emphasized to differentiate it (once again) clearly from "all." We are *not* dealing with the "all" of things; instead, we are dealing

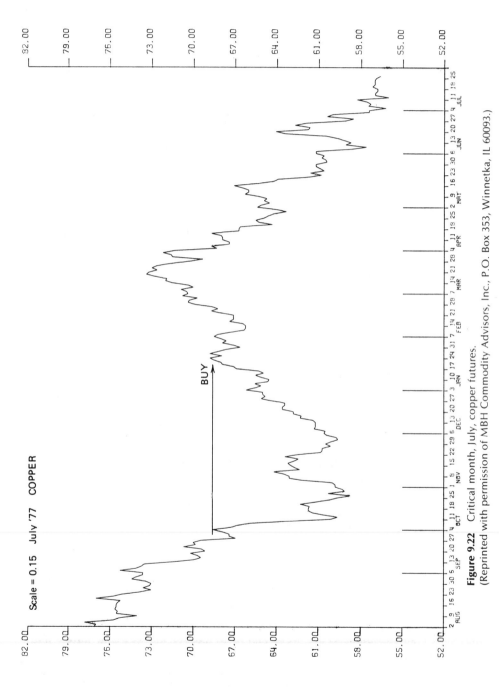

Figure 9.22 Critical month, July, copper futures.
(Reprinted with permission of MBH Commodity Advisors, Inc., P.O. Box 353, Winnetka, IL 60093.)

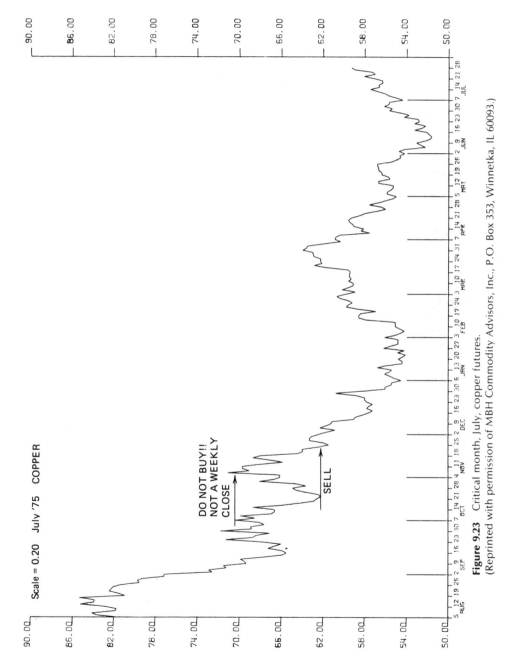

Figure 9.23 Critical month, July, copper futures.
(Reprinted with permission of MBH Commodity Advisors, Inc., P.O. Box 353, Winnetka, IL 60093.)

141

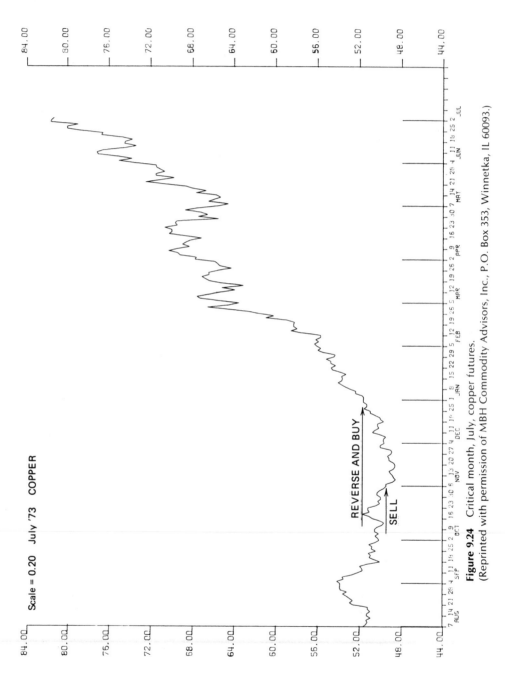

Figure 9.24 Critical month, July, copper futures.
(Reprinted with permission of MBH Commodity Advisors, Inc., P.O. Box 353, Winnetka, IL 60093.)

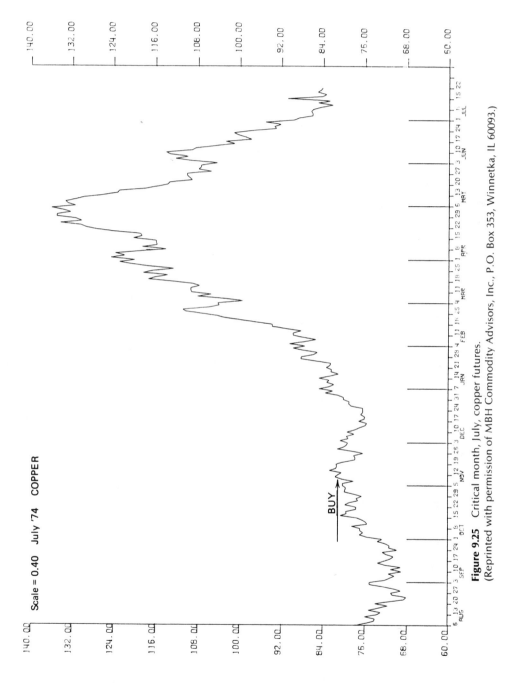

Figure 9.25 Critical month, July, copper futures.
(Reprinted with permission of MBH Commodity Advisors, Inc., P.O. Box 353, Winnetka, IL 60093.)

143

Copper tends to move higher if prices penetrate October highs.

CHECKLIST:
Watch July futures contract
Determine high and low for month of October
Buy weekly close above October high
Sell weekly close below October low

RISK

risk becomes other extreme for month of October

RELIABILITY

high historical reliability

Figure 9.26   Critical month concepts in copper.

with the "most" of things—this, as noted earlier, is the essence of market analysis. It seeks to tilt the odds in favor of the investor or speculator knowing full well that 100% accuracy can rarely, if ever, be achieved.

I discovered key seasonal dates by accident one day while running a computer program on seasonal tendencies. I noticed that gold futures were prone in most years to make a rather large up move from mid-August to mid-September. I was not too concerned with why this happened; instead, I was interested in determining how well I could fine tune the entry and exit dates to see whether there was some correlation from year to year. With the aid of the computer I embarked on an iterative process by which many hypothetical entry and exit dates could be studied throughout a period of many years. Entry and exit as short as one day to as long as 12 months could be tested. In practice literally billions of calculations would have to be tested and studied to arrive at an optimum overlap. Figure 9.32 shows schematically how the data was searched for key dates. As you can see, the process would have taken almost a lifetime if done by hand.

What emerged after the process was completed on the metals was a *most* interesting set of dates, prices, entries, and exits. Figures 9.33, 9.34, 9.35, and 9.36 show a few of the important key seasonals in several of the metals. The tables show entry date price, exit date price, profit/loss, and cumulative profit/loss. The simple rules used in calculating the key seasonals were as follows:

1.   Market was entered and exited on close of trading.
2.   If market was closed on key date, then entry was made next day on the close.
3.   Each seasonal carried with it a risk point used for testing. The risk point was generally set as a given percentage of entry price.
4.   News, fundamentals, and so on were totally ignored.

The results of this intensive research effort were exceptionally rewarding. Hundreds of entry and exit dates were tested on each calendar year. Many dif-

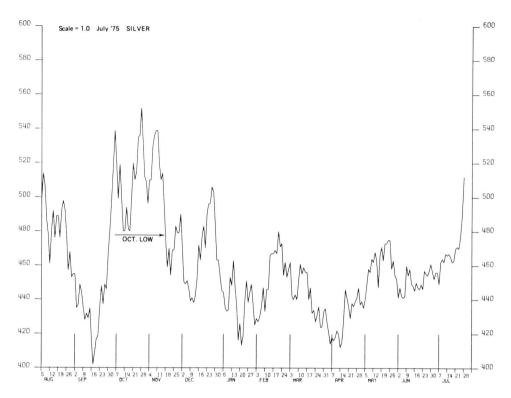

Figure 9.27 Critical month in silver.
(Reprinted with permission of MBH Commodity Advisors, Inc., P.O. Box 353, Winnetka, IL 60093.)

Figure 9.28 Critical month in silver.
(Reprinted with permission of MBH Commodity Advisors, Inc., P.O. Box 353, Winnetka, IL 60093.)

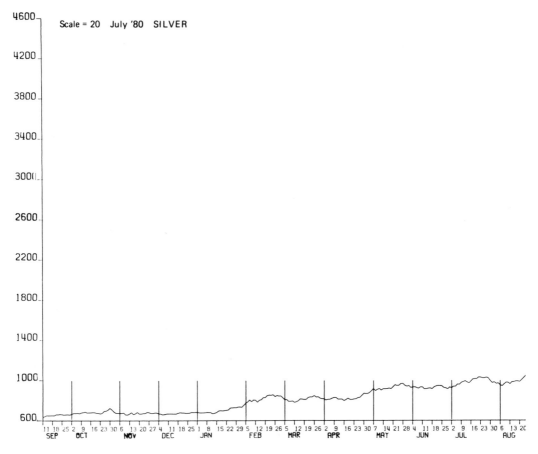

Figure 9.29 Critical month in silver.
(Reprinted with permission of MBH Commodity Advisors, Inc., P.O. Box 353, Winnetka, IL 60093.)

146

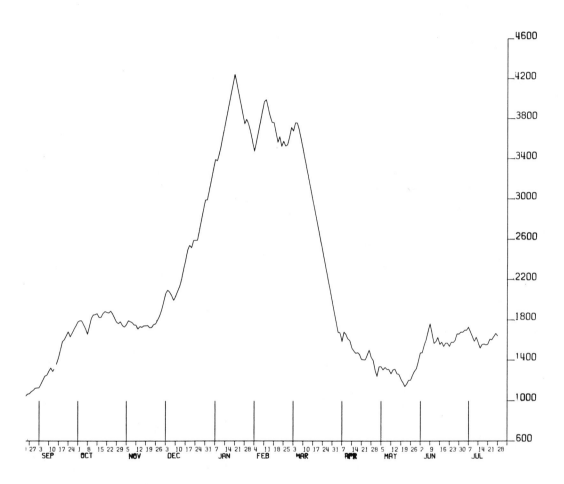

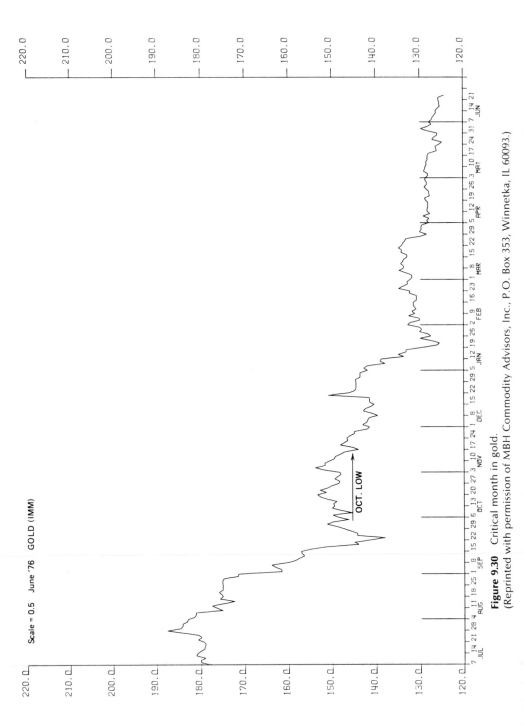

Figure 9.30 Critical month in gold.
(Reprinted with permission of MBH Commodity Advisors, Inc., P.O. Box 353, Winnetka, IL 60093.)

ferent levels of risk were examined. The data I have available is voluminous. In fact, there is more than enough data on key seasonal dates to cover an entire reference text of more than seveal hundred pages. This book, however, is not primarily devoted to the concept and use of key seasonal dates. As a sampling I have included a few key date situations for each of the metals based on the work described here.

Key Seasonal Dates In Silver

Figure 9.35 shows one of the leading key date trades in silver and its results back to 1968. The same pattern probably exists in the cash market previous to the starting date of my data, as well as in gold futures.

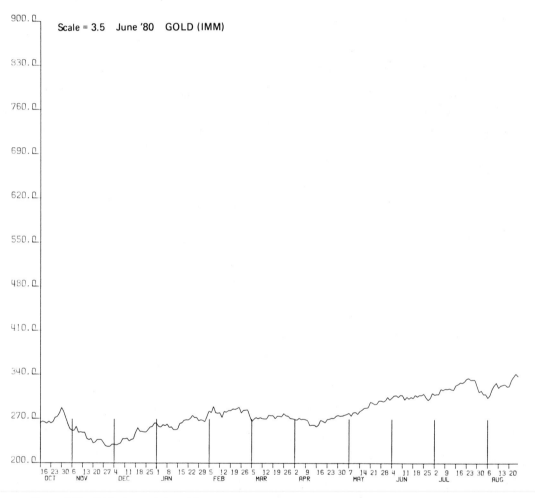

Figure 9.31 Critical month in gold.
(Reprinted with permission of MBH Commodity Advisors, Inc., P.O. Box 353, Winnetka, IL 60093.)

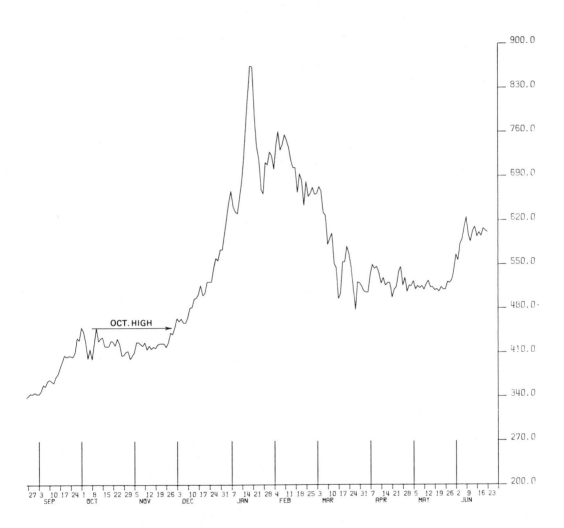

OCT. HIGH

Step #	Procedure
1	Determine "buy and sell dates"
2	Define length of time and number of years to search
3	Begin "buy and sell" procedure on given calendar date
4	End buy or sell on $N + 1$ days
5	Continue through end of data
6	Begin on start date + one day and repeat process
7	Display array of data and % up/down, total gain/loss
8	Search for highest readings
9	Rerun data to verify accuracy of key dates

Figure 9.32 The iterative process in key seasonal date analysis.

START DATE: 12/ 6 END DATE: 3/15

STOP LOSS = *100.%

CONTRACT	BUY		PRICE	DATE	PRICE	PROFIT TOTAL
6707CP	12	666	52.40	31567	45.45	−6.95
6807CP	12	667	49.40	31863	56.05	6.65
6907CP	12	663	48.65	31769	53.00	4.35
7007CP	12	869	69.50	31670	71.85	2.35
7107CP	12	770	47.30	31571	52.70	5.40
7207CP	12	671	47.90	31572	53.00	5.10
7307CP	12	672	49.70	31573	63.10	13.40
7407CP	12	673	79.50	31574	109.20	29.70
7507CP	12	674	61.70	31775	59.40	−2.30
7607CP	12	875	56.30	31576	62.60	6.30
7707CP	12	676	60.60	31577	72.00	11.40
7807CP	12	677	60.30	31573	61.50	1.20
7907CP	12	673	71.00	31579	90.50	19.50
3007CP	12	679	97.40	31780	97.00	−0.40
8107CP	12	880	93.30	31631	86.20	−7.10
8207CP	12	731	80.55	31582	70.70	−9.85
9307CP	12	682	69.10	31583	75.95	6.85

Figure 9.33 Key dates in July copper.

START DATE: 12/27   END DATE: 2/28

STOP LOSS = *100.%

CONTRACT BUY	PRICE	DATE	PRICE	PROFIT	TOTAL
6707CP	122766	55.20	22867	47.90	−7.30
6807CP	122767	49.40	22868	58.25	8.85
6907CP	122768	47.95	22869	48.80	0.85
7007CP	122969	68.25	3 270	70.90	2.65
7107CP	122870	48.55	3 171	49.25	0.70
7207CP	122771	49.05	22872	52.25	3.20
7307CP	122772	51.30	22873	64.60	13.30
7407CP	122773	79.10	22874	106.00	26.90
7507CP	122774	60.80	22875	60.70	−0.10
7607CP	122975	57.40	3 176	60.10	2.70
7707CP	122776	64.40	22877	69.90	5.50
7807CP	122777	63.20	22878	57.50	−5.70
7907CP	122778	73.80	22879	93.15	19.35
8007CP	122779	102.90	22880	128.00	25.10
8107CP	122980	92.35	3 281	81.80	−10.55
8207CP	122681	78.35	3 182	73.35	−5.00
8307CP	122782	72.15	22883	76.70	4.55

Figure 9.34 Key seasonal dates in July copper.

START DATE: 8/27   END DATE: 9/23

STOP LOSS = *100.%

CONTRACT BUY	PRICE	DATE	PRICE	PROFIT	TOTAL
6807SV	82867	174.00	92567	178.00	4.00	4.00
6907SV	82768	237.00	92368	239.00	2.00	6.00
7007SV	82769	180.00	92369	203.00	23.00	29.00
7207SV	82771	164.00	92371	151.00	−13.00	16.00
7307SV	82872	197.00	92572	176.00	−21.00	−5.00
7407SV	82773	277.00	92473	294.00	17.00	12.00
7507SV	82774	457.00	92374	436.00	−21.00	−9.00
7607SV	82775	516.00	92375	477.00	−39.00	−48.00
7707SV	82776	436.00	92376	455.00	19.00	−29.00
7807SV	82977	465.00	92377	482.00	17.00	−12.00
7907SV	82878	579.00	92578	605.00	26.00	14.00
8007SV	82779	1071.00	92479	1685.00	614.00	628.00
8107SV	82780	1804.00	92380	2608.00	804.00	1432.00
8207SV	82781	1053.00	92381	1124.00	71.00	1503.00

Figure 9.35 Key seasonal dates in July silver.

STAPT DATE: 11/25 END DATE: 12/ 3

STOP LOSS = *100.%

CONTRACT	BUY	PRICE	DATE	PRICE	PROFIT	TOTAL
6901PL	112568	257.60	12 368	270.50	12.90	12.90
7001PL	112569	180.00	12 369	178.50	-1.50	11.40
7101PL	112570	113.70	12 370	114.80	1.10	12.50
7201PL	112671	108.00	12 371	111.30	3.30	15.80
7301PL	112772	141.10	12 472	143.70	2.60	18.40
7401PL	112673	149.50	12 373	161.50	12.00	30.40
7501PL	112574	175.50	12 374	172.00	-3.50	26.90
7601PL	112575	147.40	12 375	143.50	-3.90	23.00
7701PL	112676	155.40	12 376	156.40	1.00	24.00
7801PL	112577	169.50	12 577	177.30	7.80	31.80
7901PL	112773	329.60	12 473	327.20	-2.40	29.40
8001PL	112679	497.60	12 379	559.80	62.20	91.60
8101PL	112580	641.10	12 380	641.50	0.40	92.00
8301PL	112682	363.50	12 382	367.60	4.10	96.10

Figure 9.36 Key seasonal dates in January platinum.

10

Your Metals Portfolio and Money Management

Through the years the importance of precious metals holdings as part of a regular long-term investment portfolio has overshadowed the role of money management and risk to reward evaluation for such investments. For all too long, the public and, for that matter, many professionals upheld the erroneous concept that "precious metals can do no wrong." This supposition was based on a limited slice of history and, in general, arose from the performance of metals during the 1968 to 1980 time frame. I, however, persistently warned that metals were, in many respects, no different from other commodities and should, therefore, not be afforded any treatment essentially different from that given to other commodities regarding money management.

The traditional attitude regarding precious metals can best be summarized by the following statement: "We will buy silver and gold in the cash market with the intention of keeping it indefinitely and, if it should go substantially lower, we will add more to our positions knowing that sooner or later we will be right and prices will explode." This reasoning was quite prevalent in the late 1970s and the early 1980s. Essentially, there is nothing wrong with this approach, because sooner or later almost everyone will be right on almost any issue. The only problem is that capital is tied up for a considerable period of time, not earning any interest or doing any work. At the same time, the probability is always high that the investor will need his or her capital for other, more important investments, and that this may eventually force liquidation of the long position at prices much lower than one would want. Hence, the old adage "eventually we will be right" may be wise, but it may not necessarily produce profits. For those who can truly buy, hold, and add, without dipping into needed resources, or without being forced to liquidate for other reasons, the buy and hold strategy is wonderful because it requires virtually no thought—only considerable and regular capital.

TRADITIONAL PRINCIPLES OF MONEY MANAGEMENT

As I indicated earlier, the "buy and hold strategy" is not necessarily the best strategy for most investors. Nevertheless, as I explained in previous chapters, the "buy, hold, and add strategy" during cyclic phases and the liquidation strategy during cyclic down phases are certainly viable strategies for the average individual. The suggestions I have made in my ideal program can vary somewhat according to individual investment needs. Nonetheless, the basic principles have underlined validity as well as historical precedent. Consequently, I propose the following general guidelines for the precious metals investors:

1. Precious metals should constitute no more than 20% of your total investment portfolio. The metals sector includes such things as futures, cash positions, and options.
2. The preferred split is, of course, based on specific characteristics of the individual cycle; however, I generally recommend that of your 20% position in the precious metals, the following breakdown should serve you well:

   a. Twenty percent copper.
   b. Twenty percent silver.
   c. Twenty percent gold.
   d. Twenty percent platinum.
   e. Twenty percent palladium.

The 20% position in gold can alternately be switched to a 40% position in silver and zero percent in gold, depending on individual investor perference and silver/gold price spreads.

3. Highly leveraged investments such as futures are recommended for the investor who can afford and benefit (tax-wise) from the inherent risk. Since living standards, as well as the rate of inflation and salary scales, change, it is difficult to state categorically an income level that should serve as a cutoff point for "higher risk traders." I would recommend in this respect that you consult your personal financial advisor or accountant.
4. The history of options as a publicly traded vehicle on precious metals contracts is a brief one indeed. At the time of this writing, there is still insufficient experience and data on futures options to permit an objective judgment concerning their value to the individual investor. There are, however, several options' strategies outlined later in this chapter that appear to have initial validity in a metal investment program. The major attraction of options is that risk is limited. The major disadvantage of options, however, is that they have a limited life span and could expire before the move one expected has been made.

5.   Losses and risk are factors in every investment program. No one can sell you the perfect investment program nor can anyone guarantee you no risk. Sometimes, in the history of cycles, everything does not go well. In such cases it becomes necessary to take one's losses; however, the probability of making a losing long-term trade decreases if sufficient margin is used. The issue of margin is an important one, because many traders with insufficient margin have been forced to abandon a position at the bottom only to watch it go higher after having sold out. This problem can be avoided by committing sufficient margin to each position on entry. For example, a 100 ounce contract of gold at $400 per ounce would cost $40,000. At 1% margin, the cost would be $400; at 5% margin, the cost would be $2,000. When $2,000 controls a $40,000 investment, there is both powerful leverage on the up side and potential ruin on the down side if the position moves against the investor. Thus, I recommend committing excess margin, well above and beyond the amount required by the exchanges and/or the brokerage firm. In so doing, the investor will have less capital, a smaller position, less exposure, less pressure, and a greater probability of good decision making for the next move. It is unlikely that a margin call will be received, and it is unlikely that a resulting bad decision (i.e., emotional decision) will be made. In summary, then, the key to effective money management is based on three basic principles:

a.   Diversification—your investment portfolio must be multifaceted and you must avoid the so-called "all eggs in one basket" syndrome.
b.   Purchases and/or sales should be made on a scale-in basis as described in Chapter 8.
c,   Margin allotted to each position must be more than the amount required by the exchange and/or brokerage house.

Relative to this last point, I recommend 50% commitment of the total contract value. Higher risk traders may want to commit 25% but I believe that anything less than 25% could eventually cause some difficulty by permitting an overextension of one's working capital.

OPTIONS STRATEGIES

The options strategies section has been included in the money management area since it is, in effect, a money management technique. First, we will define the futures option vehicle to gain greater insight concerning its potential use. Essentially, an option on a futures contract does not differ from an option on a common stock. A stock option specifies that you have the right to buy (call option) or sell (put option) a given number of shares on the underlying stock at a given price by a certain time. Options expire, however, if not executed by the expiration date. The options contract carries a certain dollar value and, if not executed or liquidated, the underlying dollar value of the option contract is lost. The money is then made by the individual who sold the option to you, and the middleman (broker) as usual makes his or her money whether you win or

lose. The options contract itself is traded as a security and, therefore, can fluctuate in price. Its price, however, is based on the underlying value of the contract it represents. In the case of stocks, of course, the value of the option is
related to the underlying value of the stock it represents. The great advantage
of an options contract is that it can be purchased for a fixed price and can decline only to zero. Its up-side potential, however, is unlimited. Options contracts can be bought or sold short. When one buys a call option, therefore, one
is betting that prices will go higher; however, when one sells a call option, one
is, in effect, betting that prices will go lower. On the other hand, a put option
that is bought is betting that prices will go lower; a put option that is sold is
betting that prices will go higher. (This latter point of selling a put may require
some thought, but basically speaking it constitutes a double negative). By selling you indicate negative direction, and a negative of a negative mathematically equals a positive.

It may, at times, be advantageous to sell a put rather than to buy a call because selling a put could be cheaper in some instances than buying a call. Selling a call could, in certain instances, be cheaper than buying a put. These are
only a few of the aspects that relate to the intricacies of options trading.

Now, however, let us proceed to a discussion of the strategy of metals options. Let us assume that you have established a long-term position in gold on
the long side. Assume, furthermore, that prices move in your favor and enter an
intermediate-term top area. You recognize that a top is being made, but you do
not wish to liquidate your position for fear that you will lose your base to a relatively low price. On the other hand, you feel that not to take the opportunity
would be wasteful since your technical work is quite clear about the anticipated
decline. The strategy here would be quite simple. You would "hedge" your long
position in gold either by buying a put option (betting that prices will go lower)
or by selling a call option (betting that prices will go lower for a fixed premium).
In effect, you would be ensuring your long position against decline by taking an
option contrary to your position. Your total cost would be your insurance premium, in effect, and given proper timing you could liquidate your option position and show a profit. You would still retain your investment position, and if
the cycles are working properly, the market will rise and you will have made
intermediate-term profits by trading the options.

Another strategy might be as follows. Assume that gold prices begin to
move higher earlier than you had expected. Your work tells you that the low is
not yet in. Your technical indications, however, suggest that the low could have
been made early. In this case, instead of committing your full long-term position, you would simply buy a call option, perhaps for a six month stretch, paying a specific premium, thereby limiting your risk, and, for all intents and
purposes, you would own the gold.

Finally, one could use a spread or straddle approach. Assume that you are
uncertain about the position of a given cycle. You know that important lows
are due in three to six months; you fear that they may already have been
made, and yet you know that the last leg of a bear market is usually the most
severe in terms of decline. How would you deal with this situation? Simply, you
would spread the market—you would buy a call option and buy a put option at
the same time. If the market goes down, the put option will increase in value; if

the market goes up, the call option will increase in value. In the normal spread or straddle, one side loses money while the other side makes money. The only way you can lose is if the market fails to make a major move in either direction prior to the expiration of the options contract. Of course, all the situations described above can be reversed in bear markets. Many other possible combinations also exist and numerous studies will undoubtedly be published on futures options in the metals, since their potential for leverage and for limited risk is immense. In the area of stock options, many studies have been done on premiums, discounts, and relationships to underlying securities and no doubt similar information will, at some point, be available on futures options.

11

Metal Spreads and Repetitive Patterns

Much of this chapter is taken verbatim from my previous book *How to Profit From Seasonal Commodity Spreads* (John Wiley & Sons: 1983).* The information is highly relevant to metals but did not require duplication of effort by rewriting. Therefore, it was taken directly from the above cited book. My thanks of John Wiley and Sons for permission to quote and reprint extensively.

In addition to the cyclic and seasonal factors discussed in previous chapters, several interesting and repetitive patterns also exist in metal spreads. A full discussion of seasonal spread factors is contained in *How to Profit from Seasonal Commodity Spreads*. In addition to the traditional seasonal patterns that exist primarily in copper srpeads, there are also relative value spread patterns that have distinct properties in bull and bear markets. Before discussing these patterns, however, I will briefly review background information on spreads in general, some of this information was extracted from *How to Profit from Seasonal Commodity Spreads*.

The commodity spread as a speculative vehicle is frequently ignored by commodity traders. In the past it was considered the domain of the professional. This is an unfortunate situation since commodity spreads have greater profit potential and higher reliability than do net positions in the commodity market. For a variety of reasons discussed in this book, the spread has been either overlooked or avoided. My intention in writing this chapter is primarily to educate all interested parties in the characteristics of metal spreads. In other

---

* J. Bernstein, *How to Profit From Seasonal Commodity Spreads.* (New York: Wiley, 1983).

words, it is my contention that there exists a cyclic or seasonal tendency in metal spreads and that this tendency can be used to the profit advantage of a speculator or trader.

Although the novice trader may acquire some understanding of the spread, its functions, and its working relationships from this book, I stress that the spread is not my primary concern. The area of seasonal analysis, however, is given considerably more attention. For anyone who is unfamiliar with seasonals, this book can provide a reasonably good starting point. There are several other sources that will give you better understanding of seasonals, such as *Profits through Seasonal Trading.**

THE COMMODITY SPREAD—A WORKING DEFINITION

All too often, commodity traders pay too much attention to the mechanics of a situation and too little attention to the ultimate goal, which, of course, is making profits. With this in mind, let us define the commodity spread in a fashion that will permit us to spend as much time as possible on our second topic and as little time as possible on the definition itself. The commodity spread combines the two possible positions in commodity trading—short and long at the same time. The spread trader initiates a position in two months of the same commodity or possibly in one month of two different commodities, short in one and long in another. The profits therefore could be made in one of three ways: (1) the position in which the trader is short will make more money than the amount that will be lost on the corresponding long position during the same period of time; (2) the long position that the trader has initiated will make more money than the amount that will be lost by the short position during the same period of time; or (3) the long position will move higher while the short position moves lower.

For our discussion, we will be concerned primarily with spreads within the same market, short for one month and long during another (intracommodity spreads), and spreads between two different markets.

Another name for commodity spreads is *straddles,* which states in a more concise way the exact nature of a spread. In effect, one is straddling the market. It is similar to straddling a horse: we have one leg on each side of the saddle. Many traders refer to "lifting one leg of a spread." Keeping our "straddle" analogy in mind, we can see that the term "lifting one leg of a spread" means simply getting out, or covering one of the spread sides, thereby remaining net long or short depending on which leg was lifted. To gain facility with spreads, it is best to examine as many charts as possible. Unless one has had considerable exposure to spreads, the mechanics can become confusing. There is a tendency to reverse the premiums and/or discounts, and only experience can help you avoid this common difficulty.

---

* J. Grushcow and C. Smith, *Profits Through Seasonal Trading* (New York: John Wiley & Sons, 1980).

SPREADS—WHY TRADE THEM?

For many years, the commodity spread has not been given sufficient attention as a profit-making vehicle, because few traders understand commodity spreads and fewer yet are willing to take the time to learn. Nevertheless, experience has shown that an understanding of commodity spread relationships can be a valuable tool in analyzing the technical and fundamental situation underlying any market. Many traders believe that being in two positions at any one time places them in a position of double jeopardy. Realizing the ultimate fear in this case would be both legs of the spread working against the trader at the same time. Although this does and will happen, it is most certainly not a valid reason for avoiding the spread market. The other side of the coin, naturally, is both legs of the spread working in favor of the trader. It boils down to a question of risk. It is my opinion that a well-selected spread portfolio entails considerably less overall risk than does a portfolio limited strictly to net positions.

A second factor relating to the relatively infrequent use of spreads is the historical dominance of commercial interests in the spread market. This factor perhaps has made many traders unjustifiably afraid of the market. These same traders, however, are willing to trade net positions whenever commercial dominance and influences are equally prevalent. Another excuse frequently cited by traders for their lack of interest in spreads is the fear that getting into or out of a spread may be an especially difficult undertaking. This is not the case, either. Getting into and out of spreads is a relatively simple, easily understood procedure. The use of market orders per se is not necessarily an advisable technique; however, placing orders at predetermined prices is a viable and effective methodology. A fourth excuse for not trading spreads, and perhaps the most frequent, is plain and simple ignorance. Such ignorance extends not only to the actual workings of spread relationships, but also to the typical action of various commodity spreads under different market conditions. It is to this last aspect that our study is addressed. Clearly I will not be successful in educating all readers in the finer details of commodity spread trading. If I can help you achieve a general understanding of seasonal behavior within commodity spreads, however, I will consider my task to have been accomplished.

THE CONCEPT OF SEASONALITY—A BRIEF REFRESHER

Seasonality has already been discussed in Chapter 9. As you know, commodity markets are subject to the influence of natural events. The single most significant factor affecting commodity prices, particularly in the agricultural sector, is weather. It would, therefore, be natural to assume that the price relationships in a market would follow a more or less seasonal pattern similar to the one dictated by nature.

The grain markets are understandably seasonal in their price fluctuations. In addition, the meat and livestock markets have exhibited seasonal price tendencies for many years. It is probably true that seasonal price tendencies have existed since the beginning of trade and barter as we know it. It is also true that seasonality in underlying markets necessarily leads to seasonality in spread relationships. Seasonals also exist in metal spreads.

Most important, seasonal price and spread tendencies are reasonably predictable; thus, they can be used as tools for the producer, consumer, and speculator. Since repetition is the basis for most, if not all, price and trend forecasting, the use of such patterns is highly significant. Commercial interests are well aware of the existent patterns, and they capitalize on these virtually every day in their dealings with the producer. The manner in which crops are marketed to the grain elevator or large merchandiser reflects seasonal fluctuations in prices due to many factors, most of which are a direct function of seasonal variation.

Hence, the concept of seasonality is valid from an historical and experimental standpoint, and it is also a fact that cannot and should not be ignored by the aspiring speculator. The current study is designed to take seasonal price movements beyond the cash market, beyond the net futures market, and into the realm of spread movement. To prepare yourself, I suggest you obtain a clear understanding of this concept if you have not already done so. Any of the relevant texts recommended on my reading list (Appendix I) will suffice.

MARKET ENTRY AND EXIT: TYPES OF ORDERS

Market entry is always a chore requiring knowledge as well as a touch of artistic input. The text that accompanies each spread situation in Figures 11.7 to 11.14 gives you an idea of the optimum entry time. Spread charts and timing can give you a more complete understanding of precisely when spread trades should be established. Technical guidelines are a necessary part of commodity trading; however, the most difficult part of any trading, whether spread or net position, is actual market entry. For a variety of reasons, both psychological and technical, order placement becomes the greatest single obstacle standing in the way of successful trading. The time that elapses from actual signal to market entry is critical. There are several ways in which spreads can be entered; each has its own advantages and disadvantages. Here are a few of my definitions and observations.

1. *Entry at the Market.* The most certain way to establish a spread or net position is to enter at the market. Although this procedure may not cause problems in most net positions, it can account for especially poor price fills in spreads. To appreciate how spread price fills can be especially poor when done "at the market," it is important to understand how the floor trader executing a spread order fulfills his or her obligation. Since most pit brokers (floor traders) are extremely busy, and since they cannot be in two places in the pit at once, it is not necessary for them to shop around for the best possible spread price. If an order is given to them at the market and market volume is especially thin (low), they will simply execute at the going price. When the market is thinly traded, the going price on the long side will be higher than what you expected, and the going price on the short side will be lower than what you expected. Hence, you can come out behind in two ways. Instead of receiving just one poor

price fill, as you might in a net position, you will end up with two poor price fills at a spread differential that is usually not close to what you expected. The thinner the market, the more likely a poor fill. Whether entering or exiting a market, I would use market orders as my last choice. It is, in my opinion, a desperation order, something I call an LMO ("Let Me Out").

The only advantage of a market order is that it guarantees you a position no matter what. There are a few conditions, however, under which a market order would be advisable. If, for example, you have missed an ideal opportunity to enter a given spread, or to exit a given spread, then a market order might be justified. If you have carried a spread position into the delivery period and it is absolutely necessary to liquidate to avoid delivery, then a market order is justified. In any event, my rule of thumb is that entry at the market or exit at the market almost always guarantees you a poor price fill, so do not be surprised; it is certainly not your broker's fault.

2. *Legging In and Legging Out.* A common but not necessarily wise procedure for spread entry and exit is the legging in and legging out procedure. As the term implies, this technique involves entering a spread one side or leg at a time or exiting a spread one side or leg at a time. Typically, a spread is legged into or out of by traders who have been carrying a net position that went against them and who then spread the position up to avoid further loss. Hence, they have legged into a spread many times with good reason. When it is time to close out one side of the spread they leg out. This is a technique that I do not recommend for initial spread entry. I believe that it not only complicates matters, but also increases the risk of losses.

3. *Spread Entry on Price Orders.* The method of entering spreads that makes the most sense to me is entering on a price order. In other words, you simply place an order with the broker to establish a spread at a specific premium or discount and wait for the order to be filled. The advantage of this technique is, of course, that you will not enter a spread at a price different from what you expected. The single greatest disadvantage is that your order may not get filled. If you place your order at too ambitious an entry price (if you are trying to save money) and expect the market to come to you, you may be disappointed and, in fact, may miss the entire move. On the other hand, if you decide to enter at the market, you may give up a good percentage of your potential profit simply in poor order fills. Order placement at specific prices is as much an art as it is a science. What I have attempted to do with the spread analyses in Figures 11.7–11.14 is provide you with a time frame within which spreads should be entered. The science or art of an actual entry I will leave to you.

There are timing indicators for spreads. They will give you some ideas about order placement, but unfortunately I cannot answer all of those questions in this text due to space limitations. My advice would be as follows: If you are seeking to enter a spread that has historically limited potential, then you must be as conservative as possible, placing orders at reasonable entry levels, and exiting the market at the best possible price. If, for example, the potential profit is $300 and $50 is given up on poor entry, another $50 given up on poor exit, and an additional $50 given to brokerage commissions, then exactly one-half of your potential profit has been thrown away. On the other hand, a spread worth several thousand dollars' worth of potential need not be entered as conservatively as the first situation described. Looking at $1,000 in potential profits, one could certainly give away as much as $300 and still retain 70% of the original expectation. This is why order placement must always be carried out with consideration of the other factors described here. In the analyses that follow, I will provide specific details about order placement, market entry, and market exit.

THE MEANING OF SEASONAL PROBABILITY READINGS

The most significant aspect of my contribution to the study of seasonal commodity spreads is the use of a weekly probability reading for each spread that has been analyzed. The percentage probability reading, as discussed earlier, is an indication of what has happened in the past. In most cases, the spreads analyzed in this text extend through the 1982–1983 period and as far back as 1967 for the beginning of their data base. The longer the data base, the more significant the percentage reading. Let us say, for example, that you studied July/December copper for five years. Let us also assume that during the five year period under study, July copper gained over December copper during the month of December 80% of the time (i.e., four years out of the five years under study). At first glance, the 80% reading during a five year period is not sufficient to make a strong statement about the spread. Certainly, an 80% reading during a 10 year period would carry considerably more weight, and an 80% reading during a 15 or 20 year time span would be even more significant. Those futures markets that have been actively traded for many years, such as grain and livestock, have reliability readings that mean more from a statistical standpoint than do those markets, such as gold and/or treasury bill futures, that have been traded actively for only a limited number of years. If you compare an 80% reading for a given spread in gold with an eight year data base to an 80% reading for soybeans with a 14 year data base, the latter would be considerably more favorable. It is my advice, therefore, that you consider these facts in employing the seasonal probability readings for metal spreads.

The single most important aspect of seasonal probability readings is this: The probability readings are only an *indication* of what has happened in the past. They do not in any way guarantee that it will happen again in the future in the same way, or at the same time of year. But this is a limitation inherent in all forecasting. Any technical commodity method, any method of econometric analysis, or any method of statistical analysis that extrapolates from the limited data makes the underlying assumption that a trend that has been strong in the past is more likely to continue in the future than is a trend that has shown no definitive signs of regularity in the past. It may seem like a relatively minor point, but it is something which, in my opinon, deserves your attention. I, for one, would be more willing to place my money on 80 or 90% seasonal probability than I would on 40 or 50% seasonal probability, because I believe regularity in the markets is discernible from historical behavior. This is an underlying assumption, which, if incorrect, would invalidate most technical market analyses. My point is this: The seasonal probability readings associated with each week shown on the composite seasonal charts are indications of the past and not the future. To the extent that we believe the past can predict the future, especially when the past has shown a distinct and highly reliable pattern, we must believe in the validity of the seasonal readings. The higher a percentage reading, the higher the probability that the trend will continue into the future. As the years go by and more data are accumulated without a negation of the seasonal percentage (reliability reading) or, in fact, an increase in the percentage reading, the more valid will be our assumption. I have drawn this distinction to dispel the impression that what I am offering here is a surefire, guaranteed profit-making technique. I don't know of any such guaranteed method in the commodity market.

The percentage reliability readings are not different from the reliability readings or percentages associated with any form of statistical analysis. There is and will always continue to be risk, no matter how high a percentage reading may be. I urge you, above all, to remember this fact in your study of the seasonal spreads outlined here.

THE CONCEPT OF SEASONAL RUN

During my many years of research into net and seasonal spread relationships, it became quite clear that within seasonal tendencies themselves there were brief periods of time during which the seasonal itself was particularly strong. When I say strong I mean, of course, reliable, either in the plus or minus direction. A seasonal spread might, for example, show especially reliable trends from February through June. The probability readings (weekly basis) for the entire five month period might reveal that perhaps 8–10 weeks show high (above 70%) reliability readings. These weeks are, of course, significant for the short-term trader and can be used quite successfully. Every now and then, several such high reliability readings occur during a relatively compressed time span. In a spread, for example, that showed seasonal strength from February through June, one might find a series of high percentage readings during the February–March period. Let us assume that the seasonal, in this case, was a positive or bullish one, showing an up trend for February and March. The characteristics that of a seasonal run are quite specific. Operationally, I define such a run as any continuous time period during which 65% or more of the individual seasonal reliability readings equal or exceed the 65% level. Please note that on our charts this figure will translate into percentage reliability readings that are 35% or under in the case of seasonal down trends. No mixed trends are accepted. In other words, the following string of percentage reliability readings would qualify as a seasonal run: 72%, 50%, 68%, 57%, 83%, 47%, 91%, 87%, 17%, 70%, 67%, 23%, and 82%. You can see that this string of percentage reliabilities has a high number of readings (above 65% or higher). If, however, the data series were interspersed with significantly high and low readings (that is, 65 and above or 35 and below), they would not necessarily qualify as a seasonal run because the readings indicate opposing trends. In other words, to qualify as a seasonal run the readings must be in the direction of the seasonal trend. There may be some readings, of course, opposite to the seasonal trend, but then it becomes a question of which readings are in the clearcut majority. Hence, I use the 65% rule of thumb mentioned earlier.

Time periods revealing extremely reliable moves are especially valuable to the trader because they indicate time periods offering the greatest assurance of profit. In other words, periods of seasonal run are more likely to produce profits consistently throughout the years than will seasonal up or down trends, which have merely above average reliability. Spread trades that participate in seasonal runs up or down are, to a certain extent, less risky because the historical probability of moves favoring the seasonal trend is high.

Seasonal Copper Spreads

Copper is a highly seasonal market. In this respect it differs somewhat from the other metals. Although it can be shown that there are significant seasonal patterns in silver and gold as well, copper, to a certain extent, is a special situation since its primary use is industrial. Consequently, it is more likely to show seasonality both on a net basis as well as on a spread basis. Experienced spread traders know that copper offers frequent seasonal opportunities with a fairly high degree of consistency. Rather than reinvent the wheel, I will borrow from *How to Profit from Seasonal Commodity Spreads* in the following brief review of seasonal copper spreads. (For anyone who is not interested in spreads, I suggest skipping to the next chapter. Before you do, however, I suggest you consider the fact that spread patterns are prone to be considerably more reliable than are virtually any other market patterns.)

To understand the *composite seasonal spread charts* (Figs. 11.7–11.14), please read the following instructions and explanations.

HOW TO READ THE CHARTS

As previously discussed, a seasonal composite spread chart is essentially a distillation of a spread's behavior during a defined expanse of time. When using the computer program that generated these charts, the time span under study can be selected by the user. It is possible, therefore, to examine composite spread behavior over a 5–15 year time period.

As previously explained, the value of the weekly percentage reliability reading increases as additional years of data are included in the spread analysis. To determine how many years of data were used in analyzing a given spread, therefore, simply examine the top lefthand corner of the composite chart where the spread name appears. You might see, for example, something that resembles Figure 11.1 or Figure 11.2. In essence, data from the years 1966 through 1980 were used in calculating the given chart.

I indicated earlier that the number of years included in the analysis of each

```
66 => 80
JUL / MAR
COPPER
COPPER
```

Figure 11.1   Heading of spread seasonal chart.

spread is a significant variable, because reliability readings are more significant when a larger number of years has been included. For the most part, the spreads have been analyzed for the periods extending from 1967–1968 through 1982–1983. The only exception is gold which has limited data history. In the case of gold, the seasonal futures trends and seasonal reliability should not be given as much weight. Additional information would be required to confirm any patterns that appear on preliminary analysis of such limited data.

Another important aspect of each chart is the seasonal pattern itself. The commentary accompanying each spread situation indicates the typical seasonal low and high of the given spread. In some cases there are several seasonal trends up and down. These trends are also indicated in the text accompanying each spread chart. The importance of the seasonal trend, particularly in the case of high probability up and/or down is, of course, one of the main features of my work. Remember, however, that although each chart shows what the typical seasonal trend has been, similar price trends cannot always be expected for each year. What, therefore, is the best way to use the seasonal trend for each spread? Several suggestions I propose are outlined in the following list.

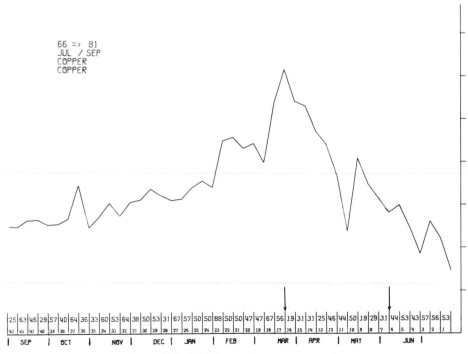

Figure 11.2   July/September copper spread.

1. Seasonal spreads containing several seasonal runs (discussed earlier) and/or high percentage reliability readings up and/or down are the best moves to follow. My evaluation of each seasonal trend contains sufficient information to facilitate making a decision about each given spread. In some cases, a seasonal trend, although it clearly exists, is not recommended for trading purposes if low reliability readings accompany such a spread. The key, therefore, is to examine the reliability readings that appear on each chart.

2. A good procedure for timing spread entry would be to isolate the time frame in which a spread is most likely to make a seasonal high or low. This can be done by examining the composite spread chart. Figure 11.3 shows the July/September copper spread. You will notice that I have indicated the most probable time frame of the seasonal low. This time period is delineated accordingly on the chart. Now examine Figure 11.4, which depicts a recent contract year of July/September copper. In the procedure I used, I simply isolated the

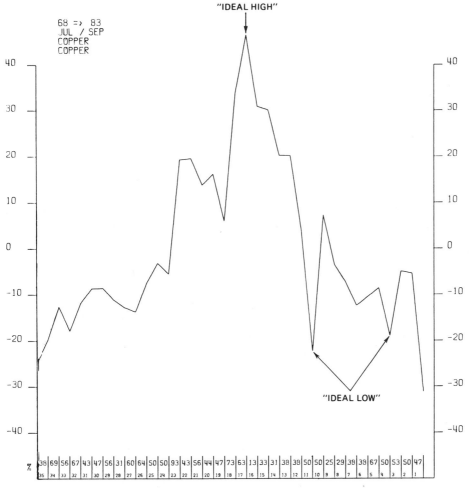

Figure 11.3 July/September copper spread seasonal.

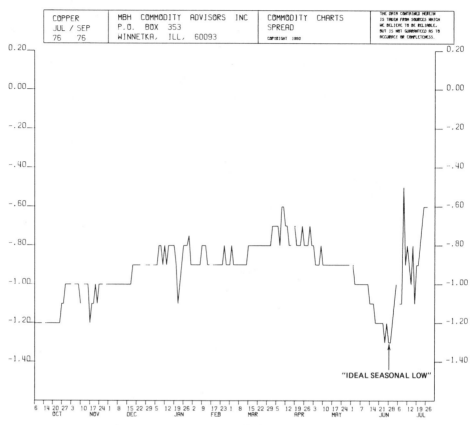

Figure 11.4   Previous year of July/September copper.

ideal time frame for a turn in the spread, which is marked as "ideal seasonal low period." Next, I examined the current contract year (or whichever year I want to analyze) as shown in Figure 11.5. This chart shows how resistance and support lines were used for timing precise entry into the spread even though the actual seasonal spread bottom did not occur exactly as it does on the composite seasonal chart.

Suffice it to say that penetration of a resistance line usually indicates that the spread should be entered. Penetration of a resistance line during a seasonal bottom period is perhaps an even better timing indicator than is the mere use of a support or resistance line for timing. This explanation completes a basic examination of how a composite seasonal spread chart can be used in conjunction with timing indicators to isolate the start of a seasonal up and/or down turn. It is introduced here to provide a backdrop against which to examine the composite seasonal spread charts in future chapters.

3.   A third way in which the composite spread charts may be used would be to trade spreads for the short term using the weekly percentage reliability indicators on each chart. This technique is considerably more risky and very short term compared to the two uses described previously. Simply stated, the method is basically one of "hit and run." Examine, if you will, the spread chart

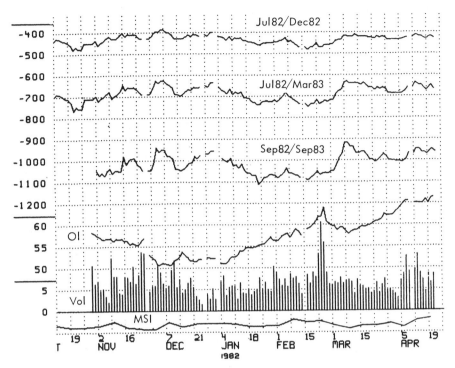

Figure 11.5   Current spread July/December copper.
Note: July/December copper was used instead of July/September since it had a larger range and similar seasonal trend.
(Reprinted with permission of Spreadscope, P.O. Box 5841, Mission Hill, CA 91345.)

in Figure 11.6. I have marked the high reliability weekly seasonal readings with arrows. In other words, reliabilities of 60% or more and 35% or less have been indicated. You will observe that there are quite a few reliable readings during the typical life of a given spread. In some cases there are more readings and in other cases there are fewer. In any event, such a "hit and run" technique is best applied in cases where the composite spread chart shows considerable back and forth movement as opposed to one or several distinct up and down trends throughout the course of the spread life. This type of situation requires a shorter-term technique than one would usually want to employ in a spread that has shown particularly long seasonal up and down trends throughout its history. To achieve this goal, first examine the current spread and see if it is following the general seasonal trend. This examination should require two or three months' worth of data and can be determined quite readily. Assuming that the trend appears to be on schedule, one would simply wait for the week during which a spread shows high reliability. Let us assume, for example, that week number 38 of a given spread shows a 78% reading and that the plot on the chart is in the up direction. This information indicates that the nearby contract month tends to gain during the deferred contract month (or, in the case of intercommodity spreads, the first contract mentioned gaining over the second contract mentioned) about 78% of the time. The course of action would then be

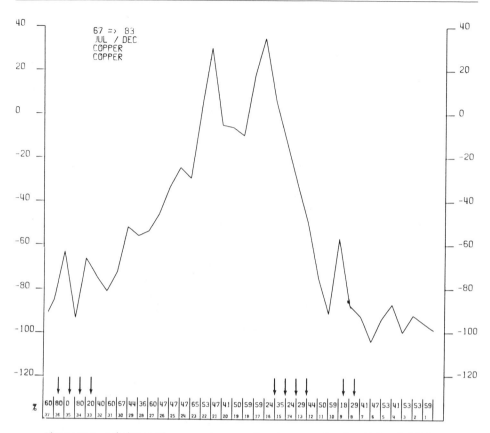

Figure 11.6   July/December spread composite of copper showing high reliabilities.

to establish a long position in the nearby contract month or first mentioned commodity and a short position in the deferred contract month or second mentioned commodity, during the last trading day of the week prior to the week of the given reading. In other words, if the second week of December showed a reading of +78%, then you could establish a position in the given spread on Friday, looking for the market to move in your favor during the next week. A second technique would be to plot the spread daily, and, instead of using a weekly plot and support or resistance line, you would use a daily support or resistance line, entering the spread using timing indicators.

   These are just a few uses of the composite seasonal spread charts. I would recommend from a pragmatic standpoint that spreads be treated as longer-term vehicles and that you expect to be given spread for at least one month, assuming, of course, that it is moving in your direction. Additional details regarding the use of the seasonal trend, as well as reliability readings, will be provided throughout this text.

   Another important feature of the composite seasonal charts is the week number plotted in smaller type under the percentage reliability reading. You will notice that the week numbers begin at the far righthand side of the chart and move to the left as they increase in magnitude. These numbers begin at one, which means that this is the last week during which the spread is traded. Week number 45, then, would mean that there are 45 weeks left to spread expiration. When the charts are plotted by computer, the prices used are Friday to Friday close unless, of course, Friday is a market holiday, in which case the last official trading day of the week is used as the closing price. The composite chart, therefore, shows Friday to Friday movement.

In analyzing a given spread, I recommend paying close attention to the weekly numbers so that your reading of the seasonal composite spread chart includes four Friday closes each month. Nevertheless, a given month could end on a Tuesday, with Friday falling in the next month, or there could be five Fridays in a particular month. It is always a good idea, therefore, to sketch out the weeks and months for the current year using the composite seasonal chart. In most cases, the months indicated on the chart will indeed be accurate. In other cases, however, there may be a variance of one to three weeks, possibly more, due to the expiration date of the contract as well as to the number of Fridays in a given month. Having the monthly divisions as exact as possible is significant to the short-term trader who attempts to use weekly seasonal probability for the "hit and run" technique mentioned earlier. For the spread trader interested in the major trend and in major trend changes, however, the weekly numbers themselves, as well as the monthly divisions, although important in terms of timing, will not be as important in terms of exactness since the long-term spread trader is looking only for general time frames within which to watch for timing signals in a given spread. I recommend, however, that you examine each spread to ascertain whether the overall monthly divisions are basically correct.

MARCH/MAY COPPER*

Description of Seasonal Trends

Here is a most interesting spread that tends to capture some of the best moves up and down in the copper spread market. It is bascially similar to other spreads we have examined so far; however, its reliability readings and seasonal run are considerably better. March copper tends to lose to May, beginning in late May/early June and continuing through the season's lows, typically in September and October/November. Thereafter, the spread turns higher, favoring March, and continues higher, usually expiring at or close to contract highs.

Typical Seasonal Tops and Bottoms

The composite chart shows a peak in late July/early June, a bottom in mid-October, a bottom in mid-November, and a brief low in mid- to late December. Thereafter, there are no pronounced peaks or bottoms; the trend is considerably higher with few interruptions.

Reliability

Very high.

Risk and Profit Potential

Average for risk and above average for profit potential.

Seasonal Run

There are several strong seasonal run periods in this spread, which is what makes it ideal for longer-term trading. Beginning in mid- to late June, the spread tends to move lower, favoring May and continuing with a strong seasonal run through week number 26 (mid-September). Thereafter there is a seasonal run to the up side beginning in mid-November and continuing through early December. Interestingly enough, several weeks later the spread again begins to favor March copper as March begins to gain substantially over May by mid-January. This trend continues through expiration of the March contract.

* Reprinted with permission from Jacob Bernstein, *How to Profit from Seasonal Commodity Spreads* (New York: Wiley, 1983), © 1983 John Wiley & Sons.

Other Information

This is one of the better copper spreads. Even though profit potential itself may be rather limited, it is a spread that should be followed each year because it has good reliability.

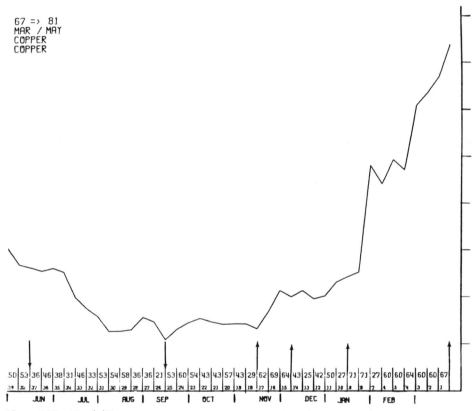

Figure 11.7   March/May copper.
(Reprinted with permission from Jacob Bernstein, *How to Profit from Seasonal Commodity Spreads*, New York: Wiley, 1983, © 1983, John Wiley & Sons.)

MARCH/JULY COPPER*

Description of Seasonal Trends

Another spread that tends to capitalize on the seasonal strength in March copper spreads is March/July copper. After a brief peak in June/July, the spread tends to bottom out, making a turn favoring March copper until expiration of the March contract.

Typical Seasonal Tops and Bottoms

The chart shows a peak in July, followed by a mid-August bottom and a mid-November bottom. Thereafter, trends are higher, with few interruptions and certainly no pronounced peaks or lows.

Reliability

Above average.

Risk and Profit Potential

Average.

Seasonal Run

A seasonal run to the up side that occurs in late June/early July does not have much promise in terms of magnitude. The second run is basically similar, showing only minor sideways movement; it tends to occur in late September through mid-October. The final seasonal run is to the up side, favoring March copper, but it occurs only late in the delivery period and cannot be used by the average trader.

Other Information

March/July copper is a good spread; however, its profit potential and risk are rather low historically, and I would consider it only marginal in terms of trading potential.

* Reprinted with permission from Jacob Bernstein, *How to Profit from Seasonal Commodity Spreads* (New York: Wiley, 1983), © 1983 John Wiley & Sons.

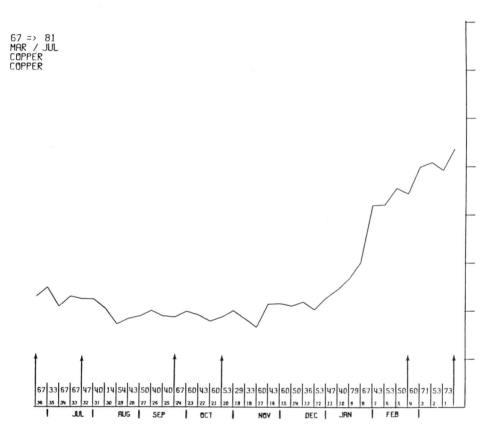

Figure 11.8 March/July copper.
(Reprinted with permission from Jacob Bernstein, *How to Profit from Seasonal Commodity Spreads*, New York: Wiley, 1983, © 1983, John Wiley & Sons.)

MARCH/SEPTEMBER COPPER*

Description of Seasonal Trends

Perhaps the best way to participate in the usual seasonal up side move of copper spreads is by trading March /September. You will note from the seasonal composite chart that lows tend to be made in September, October, and November, something we have seen in other seasonal spread charts for the copper market, with a pronounced upswing taking pace through late March. The March/September spread chart shows a high reliability move beginning in mid-January, possibly as early as mid-November.

Typical Seasonal Tops and Bottoms

The chart shows pronounced lows in mid-September, mid-October, and mid-November with only minor highs seen in between. The spread tends to expire close to its peak on a fairly strong seasonal run.

Reliability

High.

Risk and Profit Potential

Average.

Seasonal Run

The strongest seasonal run in this spread is to the up side. It tends to begin by mid-January and continues through expiration of the contract. You will note that it contains some strong readings and is one of the better seasonal runs favoring the nearby contract in copper futures.

Other Information

Certainly March/September copper is the best way to participate in the seasonal upswing beginning in late December/early January. This spread should be added to the list of those to be followed each year.

* Reprinted with permission from Jacob Bernstein, *How to Profit from Seasonal Commodity Spreads* (New York: Wiley, 1983), © 1983 John Wiley & Sons.

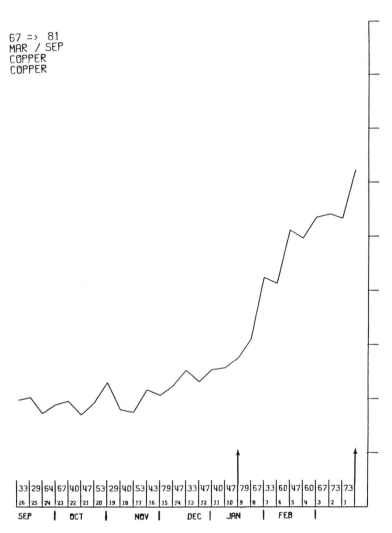

Figure 11.9 March/September copper.
(Reprinted with permission from Jacob Bernstein, *How to Profit from Seasonal Commodity Spreads*, New York: Wiley, 1983, © 1983, John Wiley & Sons.)

MAY/JULY COPPER*

Description of Seasonal Trends

The May/July copper spread has several significant features. What makes May/July copper a most interesting situation is that it contains the best of several different seasonal trends. The first tends to peak in late May/early June, followed by a down trend through the season's lows in August, September, and October. Thereafter, and up trend takes hold, which we have seen in other charts, peaking in late March/early April. This is typically followed by a severe move down favoring the July contract over the May until expiration of the May contract.

Typical Seasonal Tops and Bottoms

The composite chart shows a peak in June followed by pronounced lows in mid-August, mid-September, mid-October, and mid-November. The usual seasonal upmove tends to begin in earnest by mid-November, continuing higher until late March. Thereafter, the trend turns significantly lower in favor of July.

Reliability

Above average.

Risk and Profit Potential

Average.

Seasonal Run

The first seasonal run is to the down side, favoring July copper, and tends to begin in middle to late June, continuing through late July/early August. The second seasonal run of importance is to the up side, favoring May. It tends to occur in late December and continues through middle to late January. The final seasonal run of importance is to the down side; it is one we have seen on other seasonal composite spread charts. In this case the run tends to last only three weeks and is very reliable with readings of 21, 40 and 25%.

* Reprinted with permission from Jacob Bernstein, *How to Profit from Seasonal Commodity Spreads* (New York: Wiley, 1983), © 1983, John Wiley & Sons.

Other Information

I would most certainly consider May/July copper a seasonal spread that should be followed each year.

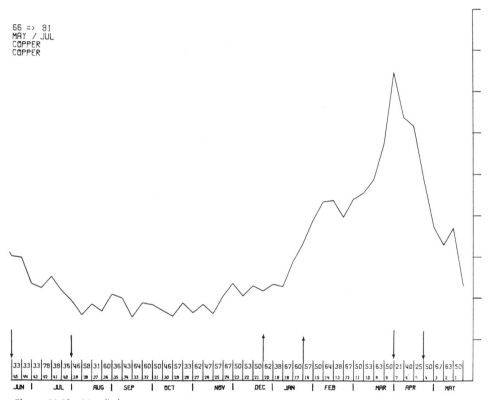

Figure 11.10 May/July copper.
(Reprinted with permission from Jacob Bernstein, *How to Profit from Seasonal Commodity Spreads*, New York: Wiley, 1983, © 1983, John Wiley & Sons.)

MAY/SEPTEMBER COPPER*

Description of Seasonal Trends

The May/September copper spread is essentially similar to most other copper spreads since lows tend to come in September, October, and November, followed by a seasonal trend up through March and a seasonal trend down through expiration of the May contract.

Typical Seasonal Tops and Bottoms

The chart shows a pronounced low in early September/late August, a second low in mid-October, and a third low in mid-November. Each low has a small corresponding peak. The major peak, however, tends to occur by mid-March, followed by a severe decline typically into late April/early May.

Reliability

Average.

Risk and Profit Potential

Average.

Seasonal Run

There are two seasonal run periods. The first, to the down side, begins in late August and continues through mid-September. The second tends to occur early in April and runs the balance of the month, clearly favoring September in what can be a substantially lower move.

Other Information

The May/September spread is not an especially exciting one, although it does follow the trend of most copper spreads. The only pronounced period of

* Reprinted with permission from Jacob Bernstein, *How to Profit from Seasonal Commodity Spreads* (New York: Wiley, 1983), © 1983, John Wiley & Sons.

importance is to the down side (favoring September), beginning in April and continuing through late April, possibly early May. I would add May/September copper to my list of spreads to follow each year and would most definitely consider buying September against short May contracts beginning in April or possibly late March.

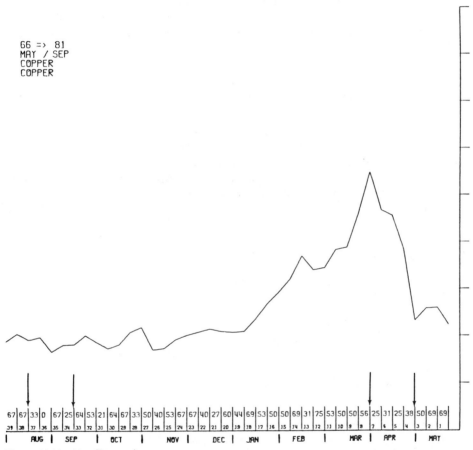

```
66 => 81
MAY / SEP
COPPER
COPPER
```

Figure 11.11　May/September copper.
(Reprinted with permission from Jacob Bernstein, *How to Profit from Seasonal Commodity Spreads*, New York: Wiley, 1983, © 1983, John Wiley & Sons.)

JULY/SEPTEMBER COPPER*

Description of Seasonal Trends

The basic pattern in July/September copper is typical of copper spreads. Lows tend to be made in September/October of the old year, continuing on an upswing until March of the new year. Thereafter, the spread relationships tend to reverse themselves, favoring September until expiration of the July contract or longer.

Typical Seasonal Tops and Bottoms

There are several lows on the composite chart, one each in September, October, and November, followed by a pronounced upswing and peak in mid to late March. Thereafter, the relationship tends to reverse itself quite strongly favoring September copper until late April/early March at which time a brief upswing is possible, however, with low reliability. This trend is usually followed by a move down once again as the contract expires at or close to spread lows.

Reliability

Above average.

Risk and Profit Potential

Low.

Seasonal Run

There is only one strong seasonal run on the chart, and it is to the down side, favoring September. It tends to begin in late March and to continue until late May/early June. This is the time of the year, then, to be long September copper and short July.

* Reprinted with permission from Jacob Bernstein, *How to Profit from Seasonal Commodity Spreads* (New York: Wiley, 1983), © 1983, John Wiley & Sons.

Other Information

I would add July/September copper to the list of spreads that should be followed each year. Although the potential here is rather low, so is the risk, and with a high reliability run such as the one discussed above, I would certainly rate this as a spread that must be considered each year.

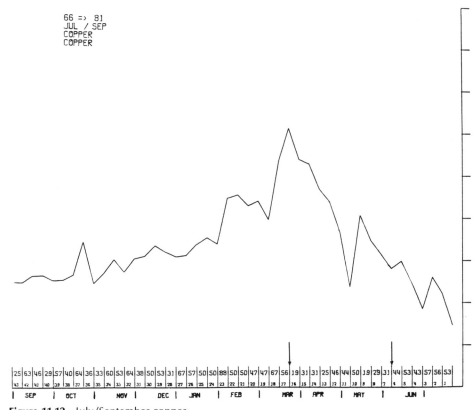

Figure 11.12 July/September copper.
(Reprinted with permission from Jacob Bernstein, *How to Profit from Seasonal Commodity Spreads*, New York: Wiley, 1983, © 1983, John Wiley & Sons.)

JULY/MARCH COPPER*

The July/March copper seasonal composite chart is included here only for purposes of comparison. Essentially, the trends are similar to September/March copper; however, the contract expires in July and does have a seasonal run of fairly high reliability, beginning in early April and continuing through early July. I would prefer the September/March spread: July/March may have slightly more profit potential during the seasonal run period.

* Reprinted with permission from Jacob Bernstein, *How to Profit from Seasonal Commodity Spreads* (New York: Wiley, 1983), © 1983, John Wiley & Sons.

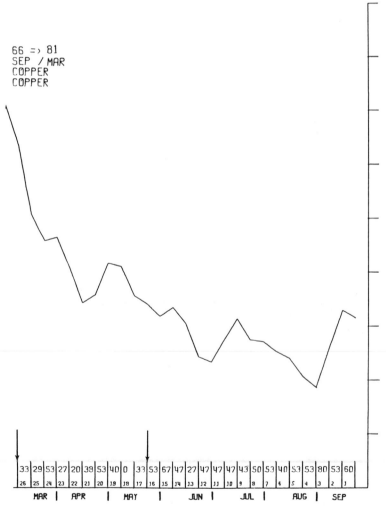

Figure 11.13 September/March copper.
(Reprinted with permission from Jacob Bernstein, *How to Profit from Seasonal Commodity Spreads*, New York: Wiley, 1983, © 1983, John Wiley & Sons.)

SEPTEMBER/MARCH COPPER*

Description of Seasonal Trends

The seasonal composite chart shows September copper losing to March beginning in March of the old year and running through expiration of the September contract.

Typical Seasonal Tops and Bottoms

There is pronounced peak in the composite chart early in March with few lows thereafter. The basic tendency continues lower until late August/early September, at which time a rally can take place into the delivery period for the September contract.

Reliability

Above average.

Risk and Profit Potential

Above average.

Seasonal Run

The strongest run to the down side, in other words, favoring March copper, tends to occur from early March through May and can be quite substantial, not only in terms of magnitude, but in terms of reliability as well. The run that begins at week number 26 and continues through week 17 is quite impressive and even contains one reading of 0% (week number 18). Certainly this reading will not remain 0 for long, but even so, there are several readings under 30%, which add strength to the case for being long March and short September beginning in March and continuing through late May.

Other Information

I would certainly consider September/March copper as a spread that bears inclusion in an annual program of spread trading and analysis.

* Reprinted with permission from Jacob Bernstein, *How to Profit from Seasonal Commodity Spreads* (New York: Wiley, 1983), © 1983, John Wiley & Sons.

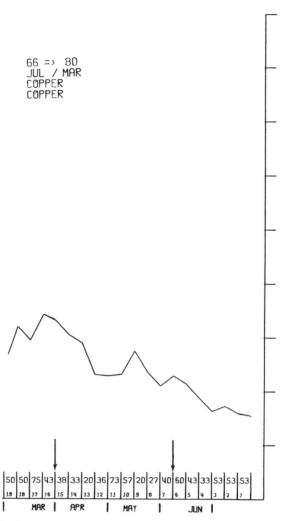

Figure 11.14   July/March copper.
(Reprinted with permission from Jacob Bernstein, *How to Profit from Seasonal Commodity Spreads*, New York: Wiley, 1983, © 1983, John Wiley & Sons.)

RELATIVE VALUE SPREADS

Spread trading is, of course, a more sophisticated, involved technique than is the typical futures transaction involving one long or short position. I indicated previously that specific relationships between silver and gold (i.e., ratios) have been reasonably valid for many years. Unfortunately, the limited history of free market price fluctuation in gold makes the computation of *valid* gold/silver ratios and spreads somewhat difficult. After gold ownership by United States' citizens was legalized, the gold/silver spreads and ratios became realistic vehicles for the speculator. Until then, data history was limited and/or based on estimates, conjecture, opinions, or biased figures.

I have accumulated my own data base of silver, gold, copper, and platinum prices to remain as free of such bias as possible. Because gold prices were essentially meaningless from the time gold ownership by United States' citizens was outlawed until the time it was relegalized, I was forced to use a "gold index" as my gold price previous to the time period shown on my charts. Hence, the pre-1974 data are open to some interpretation. I believe, however, that the ratio is reasonably reliable using the gold index. Figure 11.15, for example, shows the gold/silver ratio from the period 1947–1984. You can see that the ratio tends to run from a low of about 16 to a high of about 57. In the 1983–1984 time frame the ratio has been in the 35–47 range. How can the ratio be used by the metal investor? The answer is simple indeed: When gold is expensive relative to silver, the investor can buy silver instead of gold since there is more potential on the up side. When silver is expensive relative to gold, he or she can buy gold instead. Another strategy would be to trade silver/gold or gold/silver spreads.

Silver versus gold spreads and vice-versa are highly speculative vehicles.

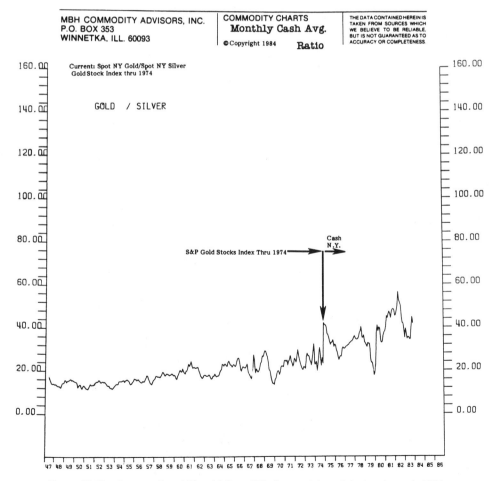

Figure 11.15 Current: Spot NY gold/Spot NY silver gold stock index through 1974.

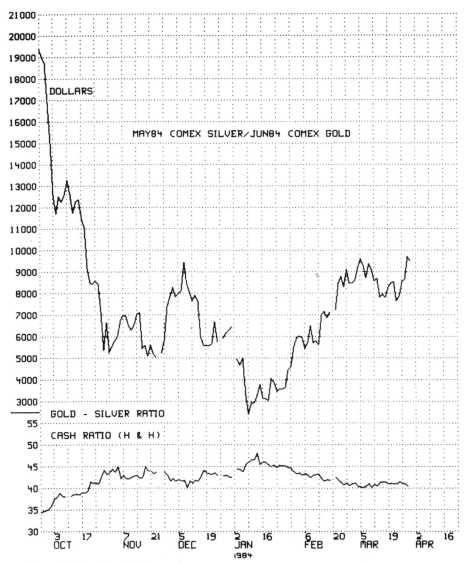

Figure 11.16   Silver/gold spread.
(Reprinted with permission of Spreadscope, P.O. Box 5841, Mission Hills, CA 91345.)

By virtue of the speculative nature, however, they are also prone to be highly profitable! Figure 11.16, for example, shows that happened to May 1984 silver/June 1984 gold spreads, and the gold/silver ratio from late September 1983 through March 1984. The scale at least shows United States dollar difference in value of the spread. In other words, if one had bought June 1984 gold futures and sold May 1984 silver futures back in September 1983, the silver would have lost considerable dollar value relative to gold. The total approximate dollar move was from $19,500 at the top to under $3000 at the bottom. The investor who had this spread on the right way (i.e., long gold/short silver) would have made the dollar value difference as his profit. The spread reversed in January

Figure 11.17   Platinum/gold spread.
(Reprinted with permission of Spreadscope, P.O. Box 5841, Mission Hills, CA 91345.)

1984 at the same time that metals found a bottom. Silver, the more speculative and cheaper of the two vehicles, began to regain lost ground on gold, and the spread moved from under $3000 difference to a high of just under $10,000 difference. The investor who was now spread long silver/short gold made the dollar difference as his or her profit. As you can see, trading the silver/gold and gold/silver spreads is a highly lucrative undertaking. It is generally believed that it is also a speculative strategy. Is this, in fact, true?

I believe that by following a simple rule of thumb relating to the gold/silver ratio, you can know when the spread has gone too far in either direction. Specifically, a ratio of more than 42 (gold expensive) computed on a cash market basis is a signal that gold is too high and that one should begin looking at long silver/short gold spreads. Then, by using traditional charting techniques (i.e., trend-line breakouts, moving averages, etc.) one can time precise spread entry. The danger of using such a strategy is that the ratio could go much higher. For example, the ratio went as high as 57 at the top of the gold bull market. For the

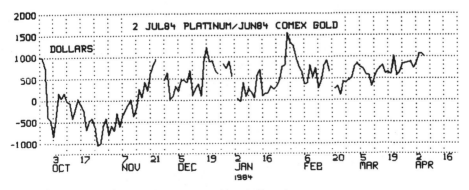

Figure 11.18   Platinum gaining on gold in bull market.
(Reprinted with permission of Spreadscope, P.O. Box 5841, Mission Hills, CA 91345.)

conservative investor, therefore, I would recommend using a ratio in excess of 50 for establishing the long silver/short gold side of this spread.

The other side of the coin, that is, buying gold and selling silver, should be considered when the ratio moves down to about 21–25. Entry, of course, is still achieved by using traditional chart methods. Historically, there have been fewer risks in buying gold and selling silver at low ratios than there have been in selling gold and buying silver at high ratios.

Figures 11.17 and 11.18 show the historical relationship between platinum and gold. Ideally platinum gains on gold in a true bull market and loses to gold in a true bear market.

12

The Psychology of Metals, the Role of Newsletters, and You

Having been in the markets since 1968 and having seen dynamic bull markets, as well as relentless bear markets, I understand the subject of metal psychology. The markets in general tend to make losers out of anyone who is psychologically weak and they test the strength of anyone who is emotionally strong. There is always a wealth of information either to support your wishes or to alleviate your fears. Nevertheless, it has been my experience that there is no one adviser, no one system, no one factor, and no one interpretation that will always be correct. The best people have been wrong at times and the last six years' experience certainly underscores this conclusion. Many of the top names in precious metals missed the top and many others missed the bottom. As you can see, the truly wise investor is the one who plays a "lone hand."

The role of advisory newsletters must also be mentioned. It is difficult for me, a newsletter writer, to tell you that you should not subscribe to newsletters. As a matter of fact, I do not believe that investors should close their eyes and ears to all extraneous input. Some advisors and letter writers have had a good record through the years. At times we have all been wrong. When you find a good advisor, one whose work you understand and one who is consistent, you can certainly use this individual as a confirming indicator. I do believe, however, that the bulk of any decision you make should be formulated from the weight of the technical evidence. It makes no difference to me whether your technical evidence is derived from concepts presented in this book or whether they are derived from other trading methods. What does matter to me (and, most important, to *you*) is that you remain consistent. Far too many investors jump from one trading system to another as surely as there are days in the month. This will likely lead to both frustration and losses.

Perhaps there will never be enough said about the importance of self-control on the markets. The precious metals are particularly sensitive to emotion, and precious metals traders are especially vulnerable to problems that may arise from a lack of self-control. The best thing I can do is to provide you with a checklist of things to remember as you invest. In addition, those who have not yet read my book *The Investor's Quotient* are advised to do so.*

THINGS TO REMEMBER WHEN INVESTING IN THE METALS MARKETS

1. There will always be contradictory opinions that you probably should ignore.
2. You must do your homework at all times. This means that your charts and technical work must always be up to date.
3. You are best off ignoring all input from experts until you have formulated your own opinions, based exclusively on your own work. Thereafter, you can see what the experts are saying.
4. The metals will probably always be highly emotional markets and you are best off isolating yourself from the news and day to day events. To stay in close touch with the news likely increases your odds of making a mistake.
5. There are many different vehicles in the metals markets. Some have been described in this text. As time passes there will probably be even more ways in which to participate. You should maintain a balanced approach to the metals markets, diversifying your funds among the many different choices available.
6. During the years there have been some cases of fraud in the metals markets. The best way to avoid being taken advantage of is by not looking for a "deal." At times, what is cheap can prove to be expensive. In other words, you must know that the brokers, dealers, exchanges, and so on with whom you are dealing have a good reputation, that they have the financial backing to make good on their sales, and that you are dealing with professionals.
7. Evaluate your position(s) regularly to determine whether you are sticking to your program. Many times we lose sight of our objectives by losing touch with our work—so keep close to your work.
8. You are best off doing your market work when the markets are closed. In this way you may avoid making a costly error.

* Jacob Bernstein, *The Investor's Quotient: The Psychology of Successful Investing in Commodities and Stocks* (New York: Wiley, 1980).

IN CLOSING

Now that the cyclic method of investing in metals has been presented in its current state of completion, let us explore a few additional aspects and closing comments relative to the metals markets. In recent years, investment advisors and market analysts have tended to characterize metals, particularly precious metals, as virtually infallible investments during times of crisis and/or economic instability. This problem was discussed earlier. I have repeatedly stated that there are no infallible investments; in fact, metals should not be considered an investment panacea regardless of underlying conditions. Unfortunately, the science of investing has not yet attained the level of sophistication that is required as a precondition for total confidence. No matter how we attempt to perfect the art of investing, bringing it into the status of a science, investing will always be a game of chance and emotion. Only by observing the necessary rules of sound money management, common sense, and diversification of funds can the investor ultimately profit while keeping losses to a bare minimum.

Perhaps I am guilty of being too conservative. Safety, however, is alway a primary concern. If the investor is not cautious and loses funds in a foolish play, he or she will not have the funds necessary to trade tomorrow. To sacrifice profit in favor of security is perhaps the greatest of all market wisdoms. Therefore, my first closing comment to you is: *If you are to err, then always do so on the side of safety rather than on the side of risk.* History teaches us that the essential difference between gambling and investing (speculation) is that the investor or speculator has the greater odds for success if risk is managed. The key words are "risk" and "management."

A second important fact is that *diversification* also increases probability of success. In this respect, we can refer once again to the infinite wisdom of history. The proverbial "all eggs in one basket" syndrome continues to take its toll on investors and, moreover, will continue to reign as one of the greatest investment failures known to humanity. It should be noted that this is yet another aspect of differentiation between speculator and gambler. The gambler is more likely to "put all bets on one horse," looking for the "big kill," whereas the successful investor is more concerned with consistency of profit and reasonable return for his or her efforts. The speculator who places all funds in one particular trade at one particular time is certainly no better than the gambler who bets all of his or her funds on one horse. As you know, another advantage of diversification is that by spreading your investments in precious metals across a number of different markets, the likelihood of your being on board a spectacular move increases. Historically, there have been many situations that have seen one market, or a group of markets, rise substantially relative to others. Consequently, it is extremely important to consider the percentage diversification programs outlined previously in this book. As you can see, I have attempted in this text to bring the metals markets into a realm of greater reality in relation to other forms of investment.

In addition to the many caveats that have been presented in this closing section and throughout the text, I have a few final remarks about the proposed system of cyclic investing. You can well appreciate that a system that seeks to generate long-term profits requires many, many years of testing. Since the precious metals markets have been active for only 10–15 years, at the most, a certain amount of the cyclic investing program must be open to change and update. The principles on which the program is based are time-tested technical indicators. The system presented, therefore, should be as effective as are similar long-term programs in markets that have been more active for a longer period of time. The important aspect of what I am telling you is that you must relate well to the methods and procedures I have detailed here. In other words, check them out for yourself on the historical charts. Learn them and learn how to use them *before* you use them. The suggestions I have made will help guide you through the learning and understanding process. The markets will never be so completely predictable that all rules will be 100% effective. Exceptions will be true in every case. Because there may be some eventualities for which you (and I) are unprepared, I recommend study and practice before implementation.

Though I do not have all the answers, I am more than willing to answer any questions readers might have. As I have indicated earlier, I am always seeking to improve on the methods and systems I am using and, where not exclusive or proprietary, I am more than willing to share such knowledge with anyone who is interested. Just write to me and I will do my best to respond promptly.

APPENDIX **I**

Reading List

Benner, S. F. *Benner's Prophecies of Future Ups and Downs in Prices.* Ohio: Dundee, 1875.

Bernstein, Jacob, Seasonal Chart Study, 1953–1977. Winnetka, IL: MBH, 1977.

———. *Seasonal Chart Study II: Commodity Spreads.* Winnetka, IL: MBH, 1978.

——— *Commodities: Now Through 1984.* Winnetka, IL: MBH, 1979.

——— *Seasonal Futures Charts.* Winnetka, IL: MBH, 1984.

——— The Investor's Quotient: The Psychology of Successful Investing in Commodities and Stocks. New York: Wiley, 1980.

——— The Handbook of Commodity Cycles: A Window on Time. New York: Wiley, 1982.

——— How to Profit from Seasonal Commodity Spreads. New York: Wiley, 1983.

Dewey, Edward R. Cycles: Selected Writings, Pittsburgh: Foundation for the Study of Cycles, 1970.

——— "Cycle Analysis: The Moving Average." *Technical Bulletin,* No. 4. Riverside, CT: Foundation for the Study of Cycles, 1950.

——— "Cycle Analysis: The Moving Average." *Journal of Cycle Research, 3* (Spring 1954), pp. 27–50.

——— "Effects of Moving Averages." *Cycles 5,* No. 8 (October 1954), p. 294.

——— "A Projection of Five Cycles in Copper Prices." *Cycles 8,* No. 8 (August 1957), pp. 214–215.

——— "Long-Term Trend of Copper Prices." *Cycles 8,* No. 9 (September 1957), p. 238.

———"The 54-Year Cycle in Copper Prices." *Cycles 8,* No. 9 (September 1957), pp. 238–239.

——— "Copper Prices." *Cycles 10,* No. 12 (December 1959), p. 279.

——— "The Cycles Workshop: Effect of Moving Averages upon Cycles." *Cycles 14,* No. 2 (February 1963), pp. 45–46.

Dewey, Edward R., and Mandino. Og. *Cycles.* New York: Hawthorn Books, 1971.

Edwards, R. D., and Magee, J. *Technical Analysis of Stock Trends.* Springfield, MA: John Magee, 1948.

Fuller, W. A., *Introduction to Statistical Time Series.* New York: Wiley, 1976.

Gann, W. D. *How to Make Profits in Commodities.* Pomeroy, WA: Lambert-Gann, 1976. Originally published 1942.

Gruschow, J. and Smith, C. *Profits Through Seasonal Trading.* New York: Wiley-Interscience, 1980.

Kaufman, J. *Commodity Trading Systems and Methods.* New York: Wiley-Interscience, 1978.

Shirk, G. "Cycles and Trends in Silver Prices." *Cycles 25,* No. 9 (1974).

Williams, L., and Noseworthy, M. *Sure Thing Commodity Trading.* Brightwaters, NY: Windsor, 1977.

APPENDIX **II**

Computer Programs

The computer program that follows is written for use on a Data General System working in conjunction with the Houston Instruments DP-11 Incremental Plotter. It is written in DG-Fortran IV operating under RDOS. To use this program on another system requires modification to make it compatible with your operating software and hardware. The general procedures will be similar, however, and considerable research effort could be spared by adapting the program's use to your specific system configuration.

Reprinted with permission from Jacob Bernstein, *The Handbook of Commodity Cycles: A Window on Time* (New York: Wiley, 1982), © 1982, John Wiley & Sons.

PROGRAM: DELTA To Calculate and Plot Weekly Seasonal Futures Charts

```
C NAME = DELTA.FR
C
C          PROGRAM TO READ HISTORY FILE AND FIND:
C
C                  1. SUM OF THE DIFFERENCES BETWEEN LAST CASH PRICE
C                     OF LAST DAY OF WEEK AND LAST DAY OF NEXT WEEK.
C                  2. AVERAGE DIFFERENCE
C                  3. PERCENTAGE POSITIVE DIFFERENCES
C


C          COMMON / IXYZ / IYDAT(21),IFILE(6)
C          DEFINE MAIN STORAGE ARRAY  'IWDATA(IW,IY,IX)'
           DIMENSION IWDATA(120,20,2),IDATA(120,2)
           DIMENSION INAM(10)
C
C          IW= WEEK NUMBER ( RELATIVE TO NOTHING )
C          IY= CONTRACT PERIOD ( RELEATIVE TO START OF HISTORY FILE )
C          IX= 1 => CASH PRICE ON LAST DAY OF TRADING WEEK
C          IX= 2 => CHANGE IN SETTLEMENT PRICE WEEK TO WEEK
C
C
C
C          DEFINE STORAGE FOR NAME OF COMMODITY
C
           DIMENSION ICNAM(10)
C
C          STORAGE FOR CONTRACT MONTHS TO ANALYZE
C
           DIMENSION IMCNT(12)

           DATA IYDAT / '656667686970717273747576777879808182838485' /
           DATA IFILE/ 'DP0:' /

           IY=0
           IGCN=1
           DO 55 I=1,12
55         IMCNT(I)=0
C
X          ACCEPT '<7>MOVE PRINTER CABLE TO PRINTER, THEN ENTER 0 ! ',IX
X          CALL OPEN(1,'$TTO1',3,IER)
           ACCEPT 'ENTER MONTH NUMBER? ',ICOM
           ACCEPT 'ENTER WEEK # (1=>4), THAT COMMODITY ENDS? ',IEW
           TYPE 'ENTER LAST 4 CHARACTERS OF HISTORY FILE NAME? '
           READ(11,1) (IFILE(I),I=4,5)
1          FORMAT(2A2)
```

```
            ACCEPT 'ENTER STARTING YEAR? ',IYST
            ACCEPT 'ENTER ENDING YEAR? ',IYEND
            ACCEPT 'ENTER COMMODITY NUMBER? ',IC
            CALL OPEN(0,'COMNAMES',1,IER)
            IF(IER.NE.1) STOP 'CANNOT FIND COMNAMES'
60          READ(0,3) ICN,INAM,IDECM,ICSUF
3           FORMAT(I2,10A2,I2,A2)
            IF(ICN.NE.IC) GOTO 60
            CALL FCLOS(0)


C
C           CLEAR OUT ARRAY'S AND OPEN HISTORY FILE
C
            DO 50 I=1,120
            DO 50 II=1,20
            DO 50 III=1,2
            IWDATA(I,II,III)=0
50          CONTINUE

            IYST=IYST-64
            IYEND=IYEND-64
            DO 944 IYLP=IYST,IYEND
            IFILE(3)=IYDAT(IYLP)
            CALL OPEN(0,IFILE,1,IER)
            IF(IER.NE.1) STOP 'HISTORY FILE OPEN ERROR'
C
C           READ FIRST RECORD
C
C           ICOM=IMCNT(IGCN)
            READ(0,2) ICNAM,IDECM
2           FORMAT(10A2,I3)

C
C           NOW LOOP READING EACH DAYS PRICES
C
            IPYR=64+IYLP
            TYPE 'YEAR= ',IPYR
            IOLD=0
            ISY=0
            XDOW=0
            IY=IY+1
            IW=1
100         READ BINARY(0) ICOMX,ICDAT,IO,IH,IL,IS
            IF(ICOMX.EQ.0) GOTO 102
            IYEAR=ICOMX/100
            IYEAR=ICOMX-IYEAR*100
            IMONTH=ICDAT/100
            IDAT=ICDAT-IMONTH*100

C
C           CONVERT DATE TO DAY OF WEEK
C
            IF(IMONTH.EQ.0) GOTO 100
            CALL GDAY(IMONTH,IDAT,IYEAR,IDOW)

            IF(ISY.EQ.0) ISY=IYEAR
C
C           NOW CHECK FOR ZERO PRICE
C
            IF(IS.EQ.0) TYPE 'ZERO PRICE',IYEAR,IMONTH,IDAT,IDOW
C
```

AI

```
C           CHECK FOR FIRST TIME THROUGH
C
            IF(XDOW.EQ.0) GOTO 241
C
C           TEST TO SEE IF NEW DAY NUMBER LESS THAN OLD DAY NUMBER
C
            IF(XDOW.EQ.IDOW) STOP DAY OF WEEK ERROR
            IF(XDOW.GT.IDOW) GOTO 230
C
C           THIS DAY HIGHER THAN LAST, COULD BE LAST DAY OF WEEK!
C
241         IWDATA(IW,IY,1)=IS
            GOTO 240
C
C           START OF NEW WEEK
C
230         IW=IW+1
240         XDOW=IDOW

            GOTO 100
102         CALL FCLOS(0)
944         CONTINUE

X           DO 972 I=1,120
X           WRITE(1,802) (IWDATA(I,JJ,1),JJ=1,20)
X972        CONTINUE

            TYPE 'FINISHED READING HISTORY FILES'

            DO 400 I=1,20
            J=121
            DO 410 JJ=1,120
            J=J-1
            IF(IWDATA(J,I,1).NE.0) GOTO 420
410         CONTINUE
            GOTO 400
420         K=J
            L=120
            DO 430 IL=1,K
            IWDATA(L,I,1)=IWDATA(J,I,1)
            IWDATA(L,I,2)=IWDATA(J,I,2)
            L=L-1
            J=J-1
430         CONTINUE
            II=120-K
            DO 440 J=1,II
            IWDATA(J,I,1)=0
440         CONTINUE
400         CONTINUE

C
C           NOW FIND INDEX INTO ARRAY FOR WHICH ALL WEEK ENDING SETTLEMENT
C           PRICES ARE NONZERO.
C
            DO 510 J=1,120
            DO 520 I=1,IY
            IF(IWDATA(J,I,1).EQ.0) GOTO 510
```

```
520       CONTINUE
          GOTO 530
510       CONTINUE
          STOP LOGIC ERROR
530       CONTINUE
          ISTYR=I
          II=J

C
C CONVERT PRICES INTO A RANGE OF 0 TO 100
C
          DO 980 I=1,IY
          ILOW=9999
          IHIGH=0
          DO 970 J=II,120
          IF(ILOW.GT.IWDATA(J,I,1)) ILOW=IWDATA(J,I,1)
          IF(IHIGH.LT.IWDATA(J,I,1)) IHIGH=IWDATA(J,I,1)
970       CONTINUE
          XLOW=ILOW
          IF(ABS(XLOW).GT.XHIGH) XHIGH=-XLOW
          XHIGH=IHIGH
          DO 960 J=II,120
          VAL=IWDATA(J,I,1)
          PER=(VAL)*1000./XHIGH
          IWDATA(J,I,1)=PER
960       CONTINUE
980       CONTINUE

C
C         FIGURE DIFFERENCE BETWEEN LAST SETTLEMENT PRICE OF LAST WEEK
C         AND FIRST SETTLEMENT PRICE OF THE NEXT WEEK.
C
          DO 545 I=1,IY
          DO 545 J=II,119
          IF(IWDATA((J+1),1,1).EQ.0.OR.IWDATA(J,I,1).EQ.0) GOTO 546
          IWDATA((J+1),I,2)=IWDATA((J+1),I,1)-IWDATA(J,I,1)
          GOTO 545
546       IWDATA((J+1),I,2)=0
545       CONTINUE
X         DO 540 J=II,120
X         WRITE(1,802) (IWDATA(J,IJ,1),IJ=1,IY)
X         WRITE(1,802) (IWDATA(J,IJ,2),IJ=1,IY)
X802      FORMAT(1X,2016)
X540      CONTINUE

C
C         FIND SUM OF DIFFERENCE ACROSS YEAR BOUNDARIES AND
C         NUMBER OF  GAINS.
C
          II=II+1

          IX=121-II
          IDATX=0
          DO 555 I=II,120
          IDATA(I,1)=0
          IDATA(I,2)=0
          ICNT=0
          DO 550 J=1,IY
          IDATA(I,2)=IDATA(I,2)+IWDATA(I,J,2)
```

```
        IF(IWDATA(I,J,2).EQ.0) GOTO 550
        IDATA(I,1)=IDATA(1,1)+1
550     CONTINUE
        DO 565 J=1,IY
        IF(IWDATA(I,J,2).LE.0) GOTO 565
        ICNT=ICNT+1
565     CONTINUE
        IYY=IDATA(I,1)
        IDATA(I,1)=ICNT*100/IYY
        IDATX=IDATX+(IDATA(I,2)/IYY)
        IDATA(I,2)=IDATX
555     CONTINUE

        IDECM=-1
        CALL DFILW('DTEMP',IER)
        CALL OPEN(0,'DTEMP',3,IER)
        IF(IER.NE.1) STOP 'CANNOT OPEN DTEMP'
A       IX=IX+1
        A=0.
        IYST=IYST+64
        IYEND=IYEND+64
        WRITE(0,6) ICNAM,ICOM,IX,IDECM,IYST,IYEND,IEW
X       WRITE(1,800) ICNAM,ICOM,IX
X800    FORMAT(1X,10A2,2I6)
6       FORMAT(1X,10A2,I2,I3,4I2)
        WRITE BINARY(0) A,A
X       WRITE(1,801) A,A
        DO 2000 I=II,120
        PERC=IDATA(I,1)
        VALUE=IDATA(I,2)
        WRITE BINARY(0) PERC,VALUE
X       WRITE(1,801) PERC,VALUE
X801    FORMAT(1X,2F8.2)
2000    CONTINUE
        CALL FCLOS(0)
X       ACCEPT '<7>MOVE PRINTER CABLE TO PLOTTER, THEN ENTER 0 ! ',IX
        CALL CHAIN('DELTA1.SV',IER)
        END
```

```
C   NAME = DELTA1.FR
C
C PROGRAM TO PLOT DELTA WEEK CHANGES
C PROGRAM IS CHAINED TO FROM 'DELTA.FR'

C
C
        DIMENSION XDATA(2,60),ICNAM(10)
        COMMON /BLECH/ IMD(24),IPC,IEQ,IW(12),IMZ(53)
        DATA IMD/48HJAN FEB MAR APR MAY JUN JUL AUG SEP OCT NOV DEC /
        DATA IPC/1H%/
        DATA IEQ/2H=>/
        DATA IW/ 4,5,4,4,5,4,4,5,4,5,4,4 /
        CALL OPEN(0,'DTEMP',1,IER)
    X   CALL OPEN(1,'$TTO',3,IER)
        IF (IER.NE.1) STOP 'CANNOT FIND DTEMP'
        READ(0,1) ICNAM,ICOM,ICNT,IDECM,IYS,IYE,IEW
    1   FORMAT(10A2,I2,I3,4I2)
        DO 40 I=1,ICNT
        READ BINARY(0) XDATA(1,I),XDATA(2,1)
   40   CONTINUE
        CALL FCLOS(0)
C
C FIND RANGE OF XDATA
C
        ZMIN=9999.0
        ZMAX=0.0
        DO 50 I=1,ICNT
        IF(XDATA(2,I).GT.ZMAX) ZMAX=XDATA(2,1)
        IF(XDATA(2,I).LT.ZMIN) ZMIN=XDATA(2,I)
   50   CONTINUE
```

AI

205

```
          CALL FIT(ZMIN,ZMAX,8.0,DMIN,DX)
          ORGX=1.00
          ORGY=.465
          AXY=1.465
          CALL INITAL(8,200,11,0,0,0)
          CALL FACTOR(2.)
          CALL PLOT(0.,0.,0)
          CALL PLOT(ORGX,ORGY,3)
          CALL AX(ORGX,AXY,8.0,DMIN,DX,IDECM,0)
          DLEN=(.25*ICNT)+ORGX
          CALL PLOT(ORGX,AXY,3)
          CALL PLOT(ORGX,ORGY,2)
          CALL PLOT(DLEN,ORGY,1)
          CALL PLOT(DLEN,AXY,1)
          CALL AX(DLEN,AXY,8.0,DMIN,DX,IDECM,1)

C
C NOW DRAW PERCENTAGES ON THE BOTTOM
C
          SNUM=1.
          DMARK=DLEN-.25
          II=ICNT
          DO 70 I=1,ICNT
          IF(I.EQ.1) GOTO 71
          CALL PLOT(DMARK,ORGY,3)
          CALL PLOT(DMARK,(ORGY+.50),2)
          CALL NUMBER ((DMARK-.21),(ORGY+.30),.11,XDATA(1,II),0.0,-1)
          CALL NUMBER ((DMARK-.21),(ORGY+.05),.07,SNUM,0.0,-1)
          IF(I.EQ.1) GOTO 70
          SNUM=SNUM+1.
          II=II-1
          DMARK=DMARK-.25
C
C OFFSETT NUMBER TO GET POSITIVE RANGE
71        XDATA(2,I)=XDATA(2,I)-DMIN
70        CONTINUE

          CALL SYMBOL((ORGX-.25),(ORGY+.20),.14,IPC,0.0,1)

          DMARK=ORGX
          IXM=ICOM
          IC=IEW+1
          IX=ICNT+1

210       IF(IX.LT.3) GOTO 260
          IF(IX.LT.IC) GOTO 200
          IF(IC.LT.3) GOTO 230
290       IWY=3
          IF(IC.EQ.4) IWY=2
          IF(IC.EQ.3) IWY=1
          DO 220 I=1,IWY
          IMZ(IX)=0
          IX=IX-1
220       CONTINUE
```

206

```
        IMZ(IX)=IXM
        IX=IX-1
        IMZ(IX)=-1
        IX=IX-1

250     IXM=IXM-1
        IF(IXM.LT.1) IXM=12
        IC=IW(IXM)
        GOTO 210

230     DO 240 I=1,IC
        IMZ(IX)=0
        IX=IX-1
240     CONTINUE
        GOTO 250

280     IC=IX
        GOTO 290

260     DO 270 I=1,IX
        IMZ(IX)=0
        IX=IX-1
270     CONTINUE

        IX=0
        DO 310 I=1,ICNT
        IF(I.NE.1) IX=1
        IF(IMZ(I)) 330,320,340
340     IPT=IMZ(I)*2-1
        CALL SYMBOL((DMARK-.21),(ORGY+.55),.11,IMD(IPT),0.0,3)
        GOTO 321
330     IF(IX.EQ.0) GOTO 321
        CALL PLOT((DMARK-.25),(ORGY+.50),3)
        CALL PLOT((DMARK-.25),(ORGY+.71),2)
321     IX=1
320     DMARK=DMARK+.25
310     CONTINUE

        CALL PLOT(DLEN,(ORGY+.50),3)
        CALL PLOT(ORGX,(ORGY+.50),2)


C
C NOW PLOT THE XDATA
C
        IFLAG=3
        DMARK=ORGX
        DO 100 I=1,ICNT
        VALUE=XDATA(2,I)/DX+AXY
        CALL PLOT(DMARK,VALUE,IFLAG)
        IF(IFLAG.EQ.3) IFLAG=2
        DMARK=DMARK+.25
100     CONTINUE
```

```
      YS=IYS
      YE=IYE
      CALL NUMBER((ORGX+.5),(ORGY+9.75),.14,YS,0.0,-1)
      CALL SYMBOL((ORGX+.85),(ORGY+9.75),.14,IEQ,0.0,2)
      CALL NUMBER((ORGX+1.25),(ORGY+9.75),.14,YE,0.0,-1)

      ICOM=ICOM*2-1
      CALL SYMBOL((ORGX+.5),(ORGY+9.50),.14,IMD(ICOM),0.0,3)
      CALL SYMBOL((ORGX+.5),(ORGY+9.25),.14,ICNAM,0.0,12)

      CALL PLOT(0.,0.,3)
      CALL RSTR(0)
      CALL CHAIN("DELTA2.SV",IER)
      END
```

```
C       FILE NAME "GDAY.FR"
C
C       SUBROUTINE TO CONVERT MONTH/DAY/YEAR TO DAY OF WEEK
C
C       IM = MONTH NUMBER ( 1 => 12 )
C       ID = DATE ( 1 => 31 )
C       IY = YEAR ( 68 => 99 )
C       IW = DAY OF WEEK ( 1 => 7 )
C
C               1=MON,2=UES,ETC.


      SUBROUTINE GDAY(IM,ID,IY,IW)
      COMMON /LB/IC(12)
      DATA IC(1),IC(2),IC(3),IC(4),IC(5),IC(6),IC(7),IC(8),IC(9),IC(10),
     1IC(11),IC(12)/0,31,59,90,120,151,181,212,243,273,304,334/
      I=IY-60
      JX=I/4
      IF(JX*4.NE.I.OR.IM.GT.2) GOTO 2
      JX=JX-1
2     IMM=365*(I-3)+IC(IM)+ID+JX
      IN=IMM/7
      IW=IMM-(IN*7)+1
      RETURN
      END
```

PROGRAM: SEASON To Calculate and Plot Cash Seasonal Prices

```
C          NAME = SEASON.FR
C
C          PROGRAM TO PLOT SEASONAL PRICES
C
           DIMENSION        IFILE(10),IUFD(20),A(12,50),B(2,12),IHEAD(10)
X          CALL OPEN(1,'$TTO1',3,IER)
10         TYPE 'ENTER FILENAME?'
           READ(11,1) IFILE
1          FORMAT(10A2)
           CALL STAT(IFILE,IUFD,IER)
           IF(IER.NE.1) GOTO 10
           ACCEPT 'ENTER BEGINNING YEAR OR ZERO FOR FIRST YEAR? ',NYEAR
           IF(NYEAR.EQ.0) GOTO 13
           IF(NYEAR.LT.1900) NYEAR=NYEAR+1900
13         ACCEPT 'ENTER ENDING YEAR OR ZERO FOR LAST YEAR? ',LYEAR
           IF(LYEAR.EQ.0) GOTO 15
           IF(LYEAR.LT.1900) LYEAR=LYEAR+1900
15         CALL OPEN(0,IFILE,1,IER)
           READ(0,2) IHEAD,IDECM,IYEAR
2          FORMAT(10A2,I3,I4)
           IF(LYEAR.NE.0) LYEAR=LYEAR-IYEAR-1
           IF(NYEAR.EQ.0) GOTO 19
           IF(NYEAR.LT.IYEAR) STOP 'STARTING YEAR NOT IN DATA!'
           IF(NYEAR.NE.0) NYEAR=NYEAR-IYEAR+1
           IF(NYEAR.EQ.1.OR.NYEAR.EQ.0) GOTO 19
           IM=1
           IY=1
18         READ(0,3) VALUE
           IM=IM+1
           IF(IM.LE.12) GOTO 18
           IM=1
           IY=IY+1
           IF(IY.NE.NYEAR) GOTO 18
```

PROGRAM: SEASON To Calculate and Plot Cash Seasonal Prices (Continued)

```
C
C          NOW READ PRICES INTO ARRAY
C
19         IM=1
           IY=1
20         READ(0,3) A(IM,IY)
3          FORMAT(F12.4)
           IF(A(IM,IY).EQ.0.) GOTO 50
           IF(LYEAR.NE.0.AND.IY.GT.LYEAR) GOTO 50
           IM=IM+1
           IF(IM.LE.12) GOTO 20
           IM=1
           IY=IY+1
           IF(IY.GT.50) STOP 'TOO MUCH DATA!'
           GOTO 20
50         CALL FCLOS(0)
X          DO 9000 I=1,IY
X          WRITE(1,8000) (A(J,I),J=1,12)
X8000      FORMAT(1X,12F8.2)
X9000      CONTINUE
           IY=IY-1
           YI=IY
           DO 200 I=1,12
           B(1,I)=0.
           DO 100 J=1,IY
           B(1,I)=B(1,I)+A(I,J)
100        CONTINUE
           B(1,I)=B(1,I)/YI
200        CONTINUE
C
C          FIND LARGEST NUMBER
C
           XMAX=0.
           DO 300 I=1,12
           IF(B(1,I).GT.XMAX) XMAX=B(1,I)
300        CONTINUE
C
C          NOW NORMALIZE TO 100. & FIND SMALLEST NUMBER
C
           XLOW=100.
           XMAX=100./XMAX
           DO 310 I=1,12
           B(1,I)=B(1,I)*XMAX
           IF(B(1,I).LT.XLOW) XLOW=B(1,I)
310        CONTINUE
           LOW=XLOW
           MAX=99-LOW
```

PROGRAM: SEASON To Calculate and Plot Cash Seasonal Prices
(Continued)

```
420        MAX=MAX+1
           IF(MAX.EQ.14) GOTO 430
           IF(MAX.EQ.35) GOTO 430
           IF(MAX.EQ.70) GOTO 430
           IF(MAX.EQ.140) GOTO 430
           IF(MAX.EQ.350) GOTO 430
           IF(MAX.EQ.700) GOTO 430
           IF(MAX.GT.700) STOP CALL GEORGE!
           GOTO 420
430        XMAX=MAX
           DX=XMAX/3.50
           IF(NYEAR.EQ.0) GOTO 500
           NYEAR=NYEAR+IYEAR-1
           GOTO 510
500        NYEAR=IYEAR
510        IF(LYEAR.EQ.0) GOTO 520
           LYEAR=LYEAR+IYEAR-1
           GOTO 530
520        LYEAR=IYEAR+IY-1
530        CALL DFILW('TEMP',IER)
           CALL OPEN(0,'TEMP',3,IER)
           WRITE(0,4) IHEAD,IDECM,XLOW,DX,NYEAR,LYEAR
4          FORMAT(1X,10A2,I3,F12.4,F12.6,2I6)
           DO 460 I=1,12
           WRITE(0,7) B(1,I)
7          FORMAT(1X,F5.1)
460        CONTINUE
           CALL RESET
           CALL CHAIN('SEASON1.SV',IER)

           END




C          NAME = SEASONA1.FR
C
C          PROGRAM TO CHART SEASONAL PRICES
C
           COMMON /BLK/ IMN(24),ITHUR,ISNL(4)
           DIMENSION       IHEAD(10),V(12)
           DATA IMN/48HJAN FEB MAR APR MAY JUN JUL AUG SEP OCT NOV DEC /
           DATA ITHUR/'- '/
           DATA ISNL/'SEASONAL'/
           CALL OPEN(0,'TEMP',1,IER)
           READ(0,1) IHEAD,IDECM,XLOW,DX,NYEAR,LYEAR
1          FORMAT(10A2,I3,F12.4,F12.6,2I6)
           ORGX=1.0
           ORGY=.46
           CALL INITAL(8,400,11,0,0,0)
           CALL PLOT(0.,0.,0)
           IPNTR=3
           POS=ORGY+.750
           DO 100 I=1,16
```

```
            CALL PLOT(ORGX,POS,IPNTR)
            IPNTR=2
            POS=POS+.250
            CALL PLOT(ORGX,POS,IPNTR)
            CALL PLOT((ORGX+.05),POS,1)
100         CONTINUE
            ZPOS=POS
            POS=ORGX
            DO 110 I=1,12
            CALL PLOT(POS,ZPOS,IPNTR)
            IPNTR=2
            POS=POS+.333333
            CALL PLOT(POS,ZPOS,1)
            CALL PLOT(POS,(ZPOS-.05),1)
            CALL PLOT(POS,ZPOS,1)
110         CONTINUE
            APOS=POS
            POS=ZPOS
            DO 120 I=1,16
            CALL PLOT(APOS,POS,1)
            POS=POS-.250
            CALL PLOT(APOS,POS,1)
            CALL PLOT((APOS-.05),POS,1)
            CALL PLOT(APOS,POS,1)
120         CONTINUE
            CALL PLOT(APOS,ORGY,1)
            CALL PLOT(ORGX,ORGY,1)

            POS=ORGY+.750
            CALL PLOT(ORGX,POS,1)

            CALL PLOT(APOS,POS,1)
            POS=POS-.250
            CALL PLOT(APOS,POS,1)
            CALL PLOT(ORGX,POS,1)
            POS=POS-.250
            CALL PLOT(ORGX,POS,1)
            CALL PLOT(APOS,POS,1)
            DPOS=ORGY+.760
            POS=APOS
            DO 130 I=1,11
            POS=POS-.3333333
            CALL PLOT(POS,ORGY,3)
            CALL PLOT(POS,DPOS,2)
130         CONTINUE
            POSY=ORGY+.540
            DPOS=ORGX+.05
            DO 140 I=1,12
            J=(I-1)*2+1
            CALL SYMBOL(DPOS,POSY,.10,IMN(J),0.0,3)
            DPOS=DPOS+.3333333
140         CONTINUE
C           APOS=(11.*.250)+ORGY
C           CALL PLOT(ORGX,APOS,3)
C           ZPOS=ORGX+4.00
C           CALL PLOT(ZPOS,APOS,2)
C           AMAX=0.
```

212

PROGRAM: SEASON To Calculate and Plot Cash Seasonal Prices
(Continued)

```
C          DO 150 I=1,12
C          READ(0,2) V(I)
2          FORMAT(F5.2)
C          IF(AMAX.LT.V(I)) AMAX=V(I)
C150       CONTINUE
C          IL=0
C          IF(AMAX.LT.10.) IL=1
C          IF(AMAX.LT.1.) IL=2
C          DPOS=ORGX
C          POSY=ORGY+.290
C          DO 160 I=1,12
C          CALL NUMBER(DPOS,POSY,.09,V(I),0.0,IL)
C          DPOS=DPOS+.333333
C160       CONTINUE
C          DPOS=ORGX+.05
C          POSY=ORGY+.040
C          DO 170 I=1,12
C          READ(0,3) AMAX
C3         FORMAT(F3.0)
C          CALL NUMBER(DPOS,POSY,.11,AMAX,0.0,-1)
C          DPOS=DPOS+.333333
C          CONTINUE
           DPOS=ORGX+.16666
           IPNTR=3
           DELTA=3*.250+ORGY
           DO 180 I=1,12
           READ(0,2) AMAX
           AMAX=((AMAX-XLOW)/DX)+DELTA
           CALL PLOT(DPOS,AMAX,IPNTR)
           IPNTR=2
           DPOS=DPOS+.333333
180        CONTINUE
           CALL SYMBOL((ORGX+1.0),(ORGY+5.4),.14,ISNL,0.0,8)
           CALL SYMBOL((ORGX+1.0),(ORGY+5.2),.14,IHEAD,0.0,15)
           AMAX=NYEAR
           CALL NUMBER((ORGX+1.00),(ORGY+5.00),.14,AMAX,0.0,-1)
           CALL SYMBOL((ORGX+1.70),(ORGY+5.00),.14,ITHUR,0.0,1)
           AMAX=LYEAR
           CALL NUMBER((ORGX+1.98),(ORGY+5.00),.14,AMAX,0.0,-1)
           CALL RSTR(2)
           END
```

PROGRAM: SEASONAL FR To Calculate and Plot Seasonal Spread Relationships Between Two Futures Contracts

```
C          NAME = SEASONAL.FR
C
C          PROGRAM TO PLOT SEASONAL SPREAD PRICES
C
           DIMENSION       IFILE(10),IUFD(20),A(12,50),B(2,12),IHEAD(10)
X          CALL OPEN(1,'$TTO1',3,IER)
10         TYPE 'ENTER FILENAME?'
           READ(11,1) IFILE
1          FORMAT(10A2)
           CALL STAT(IFILE,IUFD,IER)
           IF(IER.NE.1) GOTO 10
           ACCEPT 'ENTER BEGINNING YEAR OR ZERO FOR FIRST DATA YEAR? ',NYEAR
           IF(NYEAR.EQ.0) GOTO 19
           IF(NYEAR.LT.1900) NYEAR=NYEAR+1900
           CALL OPEN(0,IFILE,1,IER)
           READ(0,2) IHEAD,IDECM,IYEAR
2          FORMAT(10A2,I3,I4)
           IF(NYEAR.EQ.0) GOTO 19
           IF(NYEAR.LT.IYEAR) STOP 'TOO EARILY A YEAR!'
           NYEAR=NYEAR-IYEAR+1
           IF(NYEAR.EQ.1) GOTO 19
           IM=1
           IY=1
18         READ(0,3) VALUE
           IM=IM+1
           IF(IM.LE.12) GOTO 18
           IM=1
           IY=IY+1
           IF(IY.NE.NYEAR) GOTO 18
```

214

SEASONAL FR To Calculate and Plot Seasonal Spread Relationships Between Two Futures Contracts *(Continued)*

```
C
C           NOW READ PRICES INTO ARRAY
C
19          IM=1
            IY=1
20          READ(0,3) A(IM,IY)
3           FORMAT(F12.4)
            IF(A(IM,IY).EQ.0.) GOTO 50
            IM=IM+1
            IF(IM.LE.12) GOTO 20
            IM=1
            IY=IY+1
            IF(IY.GT.50) STOP 'TOO MUCH DATA!'
            GOTO 20
50          CALL FCLOS(0)
X           DO 9000 I=1,IY
X           WRITE(1,8000) (A(J,I),J=1,12)
X8000       FORMAT(1X,12F8.2)
X9000       CONTINUE
            IY=IY-1
            DO 100 I=1,IY
            DO 110 J=1,11
            K=J+1
            A(J,I)=A(K,1)-A(J,I)
110         CONTINUE
            M=I+1
            A(12,I)=A(1,M)-A(12,I)
100         CONTINUE
X           DO 9100 I=1,IY
X           WRITE(1,8000) (A(J,I),J=1,12)
X9100       CONTINUE

C
C           NOW FIND AVERAGE DIFFERENCE
C
            COUNT=IY
            DO 200 J=1,12
            B(1,J)=0.
            DO 210 K=1,IY
            B(1,J)=B(1,J)+A(J,K)
210         CONTINUE
            B(1,J)=B(1,J)/COUNT
200         CONTINUE
C
C           NOW FIND PERCENTAGE POSITIVE
C
            DO 300 J=1,12
            IC=0
            DO 310 K=1,IY
            IF(A(J,K).GT.0.) IC=IC+1
310         CONTINUE
            IP=(IC*100)/IY
            B(2,J)=IP
300         CONTINUE
```

PROGRAM: SEASONAL FR To Calculate and Plot Seasonal Spread Relationships Between Two Futures Contracts *(Continued)*

```
C
C          FIND THE LARGEST VALUE
C
           XMAX=0.
           SUM=0.
           DO 400 I=1,12
           SUM=SUM+B(1,I)
           IF(ABS(SUM).GT.XMAX) XMAX=ABS(SUM)
400        CONTINUE
           IS=0
405        IF(XMAX.GE.14.) GOTO 410
           XMAX=XMAX*10.
           IS=IS+1
           GOTO 405
410        MAX=XMAX
420        MAX=MAX+1
           IF(MAX.EQ.14) GOTO 430
           IF(MAX.EQ.35) GOTO 430
           IF(MAX.EQ.70) GOTO 430
           IF(MAX.EQ.140) GOTO 430
           IF(MAX.EQ.350) GOTO 430
           IF(MAX.EQ.700) GOTO 430
           IF(MAX.GT.700) STOP CALL GEORGE!
           GOTO 420
430        XMAX=MAX
           DX=XMAX*2.0/3.50
440        IF(IS.EQ.0) GOTO 450
           IS=IS-1
           XMAX=XMAX/10.
           DX=DX/10.
           GOTO 440
450        CALL DFILW('TEMP',IER)
           CALL OPEN(0,'TEMP',3,IER)
           WRITE(0,4) IHEAD,IDECM,XMAX,DX
4          FORMAT(1X,10A2,I3,F12.4,F12.6)
           DO 460 I=1,12
           WRITE(0,7) B(1,I)
460        CONTINUE
           DO 470 I=1,12
           WRITE(0,6) B(2,I)
6          FORMAT(1X,F3.0)
470        CONTINUE
           COUNT=0.
           WRITE(0,7) COUNT
7          FORMAT(1X,F5.2)
           DO 480 I=1,12
           COUNT=COUNT+B(1,I)
           WRITE(0,7) COUNT
480        CONTINUE
           CALL RESET
           CALL CHAIN('SEASONAL1.SV',IER)

           END
```

PROGRAM: SEASONAL FR To Calculate and Plot Seasonal Spread Relationships Between Two Futures Contracts *(Continued)*

```
C          NAME = SEASONAL1.FR
C
C          PROGRAM TO CHART SEASONAL SPREAD PRICES
C
           COMMON /BLK/ IMN(24)
           DIMENSION          IHEAD(10),V(12)
           DATA IMN/48HJAN FEB MAR APR MAY JUN JUL AUG SEP OCT NOV DEC /
           CALL OPEN(0,'TEMP',1,IER)
           READ(0,1) IHEAD,IDECM,XMAX,DX
1          FORMAT(10A2,I3,F12.4,F12.6)
           ORGX=1.0
           ORGY=.46
           CALL INITAL(8,400,11,0,0,0)
           CALL PLOT(0.,0.,0)
           IPNTR=3
           POS=ORGY+.750
           DO 100 I=1,16
           CALL PLOT(ORGX,POS,IPNTR)
           IPNTR=2
           POS=POS+.250
           CALL PLOT(ORGX,POS,IPNTR)
           CALL PLOT((ORGX+.05),POS,1)
100        CONTINUE
           ZPOS=POS
           POS=ORGX
           DO 110 I=1,12
           CALL PLOT(POS,ZPOS,IPNTR)
           IPNTR=2
           POS=POS+.333333
           CALL PLOT(POS,ZPOS,1)
           CALL PLOT(POS,(ZPOS-.05),1)
           CALL PLOT(POS,ZPOS,1)
110        CONTINUE
           APOS=POS
           POS=ZPOS
           DO 120 I=1,16
           CALL PLOT(APOS,POS,1)
           POS=POS-.250
           CALL PLOT(APOS,POS,1)
           CALL PLOT((APOS-.05),POS,1)
           CALL PLOT(APOS,POS,1)
120        CONTINUE
           CALL PLOT(APOS,ORGY,1)
           CALL PLOT(ORGX,ORGY,1)

           POS=ORGY+.750
           CALL PLOT(ORGX,POS,1)

           CALL PLOT(APOS,POS,1)
           POS=POS-.250
           CALL PLOT(APOS,POS,1)
           CALL PLOT(ORGX,POS,1)
           POS=POS-.250
```

```
            CALL PLOT(ORGX,POS,1)
            CALL PLOT(APOS,POS,1)
            DPOS=ORGY+.760
            POS=APOS
            DO 130 I=1,11
            POS=POS-.3333333
            CALL PLOT(POS,ORGY,3)
            CALL PLOT(POS,DPOS,2)
    130     CONTINUE
            POSY=ORGY+.540
            DPOS=ORGX+.05
            DO 140 I=1,12
            J=(I-1)*2+1
            CALL SYMBOL(DPOS,POSY,.10,IMN(J),0.0,3)
            DPOS=DPOS+.3333333
    140     CONTINUE
            APOS=(11.*.250)+ORGY
            CALL PLOT(ORGX,APOS,3)
            ZPOS=ORGX+4.00
            CALL PLOT(ZPOS,APOS,2)
            AMAX=0.
            DO 150 I=1,12
            READ(0,2) V(I)
    2       FORMAT(F5.2)
            IF(AMAX.LT.V(I)) AMAX=V(I)
    150     CONTINUE
            IL=0
            IF(AMAX.LT.10.) IL=1
            IF(AMAX.LT.1.)  IL=2
            DPOS=ORGX
            POSY=ORGY+.290
            DO 160 I=1,12
            CALL NUMBER(DPOS,POSY,.09,V(I),0.0,IL)
            DPOS=DPOS+.333333
    160     CONTINUE
            DPOS=ORGX+.05
            POSY=ORGY+.040
            DO 170 I=1,12
            READ(0,3) AMAX
    3       FORMAT(F3.0)
            CALL NUMBER(DPOS,POSY,.11,AMAX,0.0,-1)
            DPOS=DPOS+.333333
    170     CONTINUE
            DELTA=(11.*.250)+ORGY
            DPOS=ORGX
            IPNTR=3
            DO 180 I=1,13
            READ(0,2) AMAX
            AMAX=((AMAX)/DX)+DELTA
            CALL PLOT(DPOS,AMAX,IPNTR)
            IPNTR=2
            DPOS=DPOS+.333333
    180     CONTINUE
            CALL SYMBOL((ORGX+1.0),(ORGY+5.2),.14,IHEAD,0.0,15)
            CALL PLOT(0.,0.,3)
            CALL RSTR(0)
            END
```

Index of Illustrations

Subject Index